At Issue

Should the Voting Age Be Lowered?

Other Books in the At Issue Series:

At Issue

Should the Voting Age Be Lowered?

Ronnie D. Lankford, Book Editor

GREENHAVEN PRESS

An imprint of Thomson Gale, a part of The Thomson Corporation

THOMSON

GALE

Detroit • New York • San Francisco • New Haven, Conn. • Waterville, Maine • London

THOMSON

GALE

Christine Nasso, *Publisher*
Elizabeth Des Chenes, *Managing Editor*

LIBRARY OF CONGRESS CATALOGING-IN-PUBLICATION DATA

Should the voting age be lowered? / Ronnie D. Lankford, book editor.
    p. cm. -- (At issue)
    Includes bibliographical references and index.
    ISBN-13: 978-0-7377-3936-7 (hardcover)
    ISBN-13: 978-0-7377-3937-4 (pbk.)
    1. Voting age. 2. Voting. I. Lankford, Ronald D., 1962-
    JF841.S56 2008
    324.6'2--dc22

                                                        2007035370

ISBN-10: 0-7377-3936-3 (hardcover)
ISBN-10: 0-7377-3937-1 (pbk.)

Printed in the United States of America
10 9 8 7 6 5 4 3 2 1

Contents

Introduction

During the late 1960s and 1970s, many countries like the United States and Canada lowered the voting age from 21 to 18. Today, 18 remains the most common voting age around the world, from the Dominican Republic to Angola to Mozambique. Even when countries like South Korea and Korea have chosen a different voting age standard (19 and 17 respectively), that standard is seldom over 21 and seldom under 17. Exceptions, however, do exist. Until very recently, Iranians could vote at 15; Uzbekistan, part of the former Soviet Union, has held the voting age at 25.

In the last several years various countries have enacted small changes in voting age requirements, though observers have yet to identify a trend. During the 1990s German states lowered the voting age to 16 in municipal elections and a similar change occurred more recently in Austria. In July 2007 Austria expanded its reduction, becoming the first state in the European Union to lower the overall voting age to 16. In July 2006, Isle of Man reduced its voting age to 16, while the canton of Glarus in Switzerland reduced the voting age to 16 in local elections in May 2007. But there have also been setbacks. At the beginning of 2007, Iran raised its voting age from 15, one of the lowest in the world, to 18.

The Movement to Lower the Voting Age

Despite the relative uniformity of the voting age, adolescents around the world have begun to agitate for a lower voting age. This faction is part of a larger youth rights movement. Many argue that since young adults pay taxes, are subject to a county's laws, and sometimes serve in the military and marry before 18, the voting age should be lowered. In the United States, the National Youth Rights Association has fought to lower the vote in several states, while in Britain Votes at 16 has served a similar purpose. While the focus of each organization is unique, these and other groups have initiated activist agendas on both the local, state, and national level to lower the vote including, working with local politicians, attending rallies, and circulating petitions.

The National Youth Rights Association (NYRA) formed in 1998 and advocates for a variety of youth causes including lowering the voting age. The organization has chapters in a dozen states and seven thousand members. The NYRA held a debate on the voting age in 2006 in Berkley, California, and appealed to the Democratic Party of California to support lowering the state's voting age. Various chapters have also worked with lawmakers on a local level to help introduce bills to lower the voting age. In 2005–2006, the NYRA supported New York City Councilmember Gale Brewer, who introduced a bill to lower the voting age to 16.

Votes at 16 is a coalition of organizations in Britain working in tandem to lower the voting age. These organizations include social groups like Barnardo's and political ones like Britain's Green Party. In 2007, Votes at 16 backed the independent POWER commission's recommendation to lower the voting age to 16 in Britain. In the summer of 2007, the British Youth Council (BYC), also a supporter of Votes at 16, initiated its own campaign for lowering the voting age. The "Votes at 16" Postcard Campaign began collecting postcards from English youth, which the BYC planned to forward to the Prime Minister's office in the fall of 2007.

While most organizations have suggested lowering the voting age to 16 or 17, the Association of Children Suffrage has suggested eliminating the voting age altogether. All members of democracies, the organization argues, should be allowed to vote whenever they are ready to assume the responsibility.

Other Voting Organizations

In the midst of the youth drive to lower the voting age, at least one organization has argued against any changes. Votes for Adults is a British website that believes it would be irresponsible to lower the voting age. Other commentators have suggested that any change in the voting age should be accompanied by a vigorous civics' program in high schools, assuring that youth possess the knowledge to cast their votes responsibly.

While neither sponsoring nor opposing lowering the voting age, Kids Voting USA has been active in creating a program for young Americans to simulate the voting experience. The program has been activated in a number of states, allowing children and young adults to participate in "mock" elections at the same voting precincts visited by adult voters. Kids Voting USA was initiated to promote civic responsibility and surveys have suggested that children, by becoming involved in the political process, have even helped raise adult participation. Proponents of lowering the voting age have noted the success of the program as evidence that young voters will vote responsibly.

Changes and the Future of Voting

The one thing that might seem certain on the subject of lowering the voting age is that most youth favor it. This, however, is not clearly the case. In a 2006 survey by the organization Do Something, 54 percent of respondents supported lowering the voting age to 17. The majority of those surveyed also expressed confidence that they were responsible enough to vote. But many respondents showed less confidence when rating the ability of their peers to vote. Furthermore, while 64.2 percent believed that 17-year-olds were qualified to vote, only 42.7 percent believed that 16-year-olds were qualified. The survey also revealed other discrepancies: young teens were more supportive of lowering the voting age than older teens, and males were more supportive of lowering the voting age than females.

Will the voting age be lowered once again as it was during the 1960s and 1970s? The youth involved in organizations like Votes at 16 and the National Association of Youth Rights certainly believe that it will, but the changes that have come thus far have come slowly. The issue, finally, is caught in a double bind: the persons who most wish to lower the voting age cannot vote to make that change. They cannot currently support—by voting for—local, state, and national lawmakers who have the power to propose changes to the current voting laws. In their effort to lower the voting age, however, youth nonetheless remain hopeful. Many believe that lawmakers, realizing the power of the youth vote, may nonetheless support legislation to lower the voting age in hopes of building a future coalition with young voters.

1

The Pros and Cons of Lowering the Voting Age

Progressive U

Progressive U is a nonpartisan, non-profit social welfare organization incorporated in the state of California.

A debate focusing on lowering the voting age has intensified in recent years, with both proponents and opponents offering convincing arguments. Many believe that the voting age should be lowered because adolescents pay taxes, are frequently subject to adult laws, and can join the military and go to war before the age of 18. In essence, society often holds its youth to a double standard: adolescents are mature enough to be tried in court as adults, but they are not considered mature enough to vote. Lowering the voting age would also guarantee that politicians would represent youth interests. Others argue that adolescents are frequently disinterested in politics, and that by lowering the voting age, one would also lower voter participation. Even if adolescents voted, they lack sufficient education to make informed decisions. Both disinterest and lack of experience may also lead to direct influence by parents on how to vote.

In the past election, many of my friends, both from school and in my neighborhood complained of Bush's reelection and why a lot of us couldn't vote—we weren't 18. Thus, I asked myself, why do we work and not get voting rights? In the years following Vietnam, people who were soldiers were 18, but not allowed to vote until they were 21. The same occurs now. So why not? I've analyzed both sides. . . .

"Lowering the Voting Age: Good or Bad Move?" *Progressive U (www.progressiveu.org),* May 18, 2007. Reproduced by permission.

Reasons to Lower the Voting Age

"No right is more precious in a free country than that of having a choice in the election of those who make the laws under which . . . we must live. Other rights, even the most basic, are illusory if the right to vote is undermined."

In 1971, in a response to the Vietnam War, the United States government ratified the 26th Amendment granting the right to vote to 18–20-year-olds. The government ratified this amendment mainly because citizens were being recruited for the war, but not being allowed to vote. Americans realized this sick double standard that allowed 18-year-old soldiers to fight and die for their country when they weren't allowed to vote. This "double standard" continues today with youth being subject to adult penalties, taxes on their income, and even the death sentence while simultaneously lacking the right to vote.

Just like all other Americans, young Americans pay taxes. In fact, they pay a lot of taxes. According to the IRS, teens pay an estimated $9.7 billion dollars in sales taxes alone, not to mention many millions of taxes on income. *"You may be a teen, you may not even have a permanent job, but you have to pay taxes on the money you earn."* Youth pay billions in taxes to state, local, and federal governments yet they have absolutely no say over how much is taken. This is what the American Revolution was fought over; this is *taxation without representation.*

In addition to being affected by taxes, young people are affected by every other law that Americans live under. As fellow citizens in this society, every action or inaction taken by lawmakers affects youth directly, yet they have no say in the matter.

According to a study conducted by Dr. Frank Zimring of the University of Chicago, he found that "Between 1992 and 1995, forty American states relaxed the requirements for transferring an accused under the maximum age of jurisdiction into criminal court," and "In Colorado, for example, defendants under the maximum age for juvenile court jurisdiction may nonetheless be charged by direct filing in criminal court if they are over 14 years of age and are charged with one of a legislative list of violent crimes." What kind of message do we send when we tell youth they are judged as mature, responsible adults when they commit murder, but silly, brainless kids when they want to vote? This is a double standard, no different than during the Vietnam War. War isn't a dead issue now either, leaders who youth can't vote for today may send them to war tomorrow. Lowering the voting age is the fair and correct way to set things straight.

Thirdly, today's politicians represent various constituencies. As of today, young people are no one's constituency. Why should politicians care about the needs and wishes of youth when they have no ability to vote for or against them? Politicians have no motivation whatsoever. Lowering the voting age will give politicians a real reason to respect the desires of young people. The words spoken before the Senate Judicary Committee supporting lowering the voting age in 1971 are as true then as they are now, "The anachronistic voting-age limitation tends to alienate them [the youth] from systematic political processes and to drive them to into a search for an alternative, sometimes violent, means to express their frustrations over the gap between the nation's deals and actions. Lowering the voting age will provide them with a direct, constructive and democratic channel for making their views felt and for giving them a responsible stake in the future of the nation."

The quality of votes is frankly far more important than the quantity of votes.

In conclusion, every person in the United States is born with the individual responsibility to be active in the political process. Without allowing youth to vote, we can't expect teenagers to care for the political process.

Reasons Not to Lower the Voting Age

At the age of 14, very few of us "kids" desire the urge to vote. We would rather go outside and hike, fish, play sports, or play pranks on people. None of us were concerned with the Presidential Campaign or even the elections taking place. Simply put, our priorities were to have fun, get hurt and enjoy our childhood, as opposed to being responsible, and taking the time to educate ourselves on a candidate. When asked which candidate we liked, we would simply regurgitate our parents' choice and reasoning.

According to recent studies reported in the *Chicago Tribune*, adolescents, defined as members of our population in the age group of 14 year olds to 18 year olds, lack a developed mindset that is necessary to make a decision based on facts. Rather, adolescents vote based on emotions and impulses. For example, at the grocery store, adolescents are more likely to purchase an impulse item, such as a candy bar for 75 cents, while at the same time they could have saved money by actually browsing the store. The fact of the matter is this: lowering the voting age to 14 wouldn't help increase our nation's political participation because the votes that they add to the total would be based on impulse and not based on facts and research done.

Secondly, let's looks at the history of political participation. According to *New York Times*, current political participation in congressional elections is nearly 36%, while the past Presidential Election yielded 52% participation from eligible voters. With the addition of new voters, such as minority groups and women, the participation failed to increase. Even with the addition of 18 year olds after the Vietnam War failed to increase political participation. Yet, of those who voted, the majority took the time to get educated based on the candidate's issues and in turn voted based on it. The quality of votes is frankly far more important than the quantity of votes. We as a nation need to elect the best candidate, and to do that, we must take time to be educated on the policies of candidates and not just the appearance of a candidate.

Thirdly, voters in this demographic are under the direct supervision and influence of parents. They are not yet independent from their parents. Thus, most of the votes that would be filed ... by students would be directly influenced by their parents. So, in turn, this bill is allowing parents to vote twice for the candidate of their choice as opposed to allowing a young citizen to educated themselves on a specific candidate and in turn vote for themselves.

2

The Voting Age Should Be Lowered

Children's PressLine

Children's PressLine *is a news service by young people that adds the voices of children to the national dialogue.* Connect For Kids *is a youth-led national non-profit organization dedicated to fighting for the civil rights and liberties of young people.*

In recent years, American youth have worked to lower the voting age in a number of localities. These youth activists offer a variety of reasons why the voting age should be lowered. American youth live in a democracy and pay taxes, but have been denied a democracy's most basic right. Lowering the voting age would encourage community involvement and raise voter participation. While critics argue that young voters lack experience and will simply mimic their parents' voting patterns, young voters are capable of thinking for themselves. Voting is a fundamental right that should extend to all.

Men won it in 1870. Women in 1920. Now, in 2005, the torch of suffrage has been rekindled by a new generation of activists: Teenagers want to vote.

Children's PressLine, a New York City-based news service operated by young reporters and editors, is in a unique situation to cover the issue. In early June, Councilmember Gale Brewer, of Manhattan, introduced a bill that would allow the city's more than 200,000 16- and 17-year-olds to participate in local elections. If passed, the bill would make New York City

Children's PressLine, "NYC's Godzilla: Youth Suffrage Activists," *Connect For Kids*, July 24, 2005. www.connectforkids.org/node/3286. Reproduced by permission.

the first in the nation to successfully welcome minors to the poll booths [The measure did not pass.].

Other cities have considered similar measures, but none have passed. So far, the youth suffrage movement's brightest moment has been Maine's approval of a bill that permits 17-year-olds to vote in primary elections if they turn 18 before the final election.

Like many 16-year-olds, Pamela Tatz, Vice President of the Berkeley, Calif. Chapter of the National Youth Rights Association, feels just as equipped as any 18-year-old to make informed political decisions. "What happens all of sudden when you're 18?" she asks. "Are you just randomly ready to vote?"

Adolescents across the United States turn now to New York City with fingers crossed. Children's PressLine interviewed several young suffrage activists, as well as Councilmember Brewer and local teens to get their reactions on the issue.

CPL: Why should the voting age be lowered?

Pamela Tatz, 16, National Youth Rights Association, Berkeley, Calif.: We live in America, and this is democracy. When women wanted the right to vote, we told them they didn't need to vote because their husbands would vote in their best interest. That's what they're telling us now, that our parents will vote in our best interest. But even if your parents have your best interest at heart, they'll vote for what's in their own best interest.

Heather Kelley, 17, Washington Voting Rights Society, Olympia, Wash.: Basically, it's taxation without representation.

Jason Puz 17, Washington Voting Rights Society, Olympia, Wash.: At the age of 16, teenagers are able to drive, which means they have IDs to verify who they are. At the age of 17, they can join the armed forces, and they can get married. Perhaps more importantly, they can be tried as adults for a serious crime. It's a double standard when we are told, "You're not responsible enough to be able to vote, but you're responsible enough to face the same penalties adults will."

CPL: Okay, how would lowering the voting age benefit youth?

Jason: It would benefit them because it gets them more active in their communities. Instead of feeling like prisoners who are forced to live there, by giving them a vote, you make sure they become connected with the people and the places where they live.

Zach Hobesh, 15, National Youth Rights Association, Berkeley, Calif.: Lowering the voting age would establish voting habits in people younger than 18. Eighteen-year-olds are graduating high school, they are moving away from home, going away to college. They don't have time to register to vote and that is why many of them don't. So if they lowered it to 16, you'd have a lot more people in the habit of voting.

CPL: But don't you think some teenagers aren't mature enough to vote?

Pamela: Well, you could say a lot of adults aren't ready to vote either. When you're 18, are you just randomly ready to vote? It's not that simple. People say that 18, 19, and 20-year-olds don't vote enough. What they're not looking at is the big picture. If 16-year-olds could vote, they'd be in high school learning about politics and government, and they're being given classes about voting, before they vote.

When you're 18, are you just randomly ready to vote? It's not that simple.

Jason: The Voting Rights Act states that if you've completed a sixth grade education at a private or public school in any state, territory, the District of Columbia, or the commonwealth of Puerto Rico, you possess sufficient literacy comprehension and intelligence to vote in any election.

CPL: Heather mentioned that this was taxation without representation. How does that apply here?

Pamela: Right now, teenagers pay $9.7 billion a year in sales taxes alone. That's not even counting income tax. Eighty percent of teenagers in America work. That's a lot of money going into the taxes that we have no say in where it goes or how much is taken from us.

CPL: Why do you think some people criticize this idea?

Anna Sweet, 17, Future Voters of America, New York City: Just stereotypes that youth don't care and that we're dumb. I know there's one councilmember who wrote an article that said, "Teenagers should pull up their pants before they go out to vote." So because of our we dress, we shouldn't vote? It was annoying.

CPL: How do you think parents would influence their children's voting decisions?

Pamela: A lot of adults vote the way their parents voted. It's not just kids.

Heather: We have a lot of people telling us that teens will vote exactly like their parents vote, but then we also have people telling us that teens will vote exactly the opposite of their parents just to get back at them. I think that teens think for themselves and understand how their decisions affect others, and affect their future, and so they will vote for the candidate they feel are best.

Kehlen Sachet, 17, Washington Voting Rights Society, Olympia, Wash.: A vote is a vote, it doesn't matter your reasoning or why, it's yours, you can use it however you want. There is no wrong vote.

CPL: Should there be specific criteria for 16-year-olds who want to vote? For example, if they're failing a class, should they be allowed to vote?

Pamela: I don't think failing a class has anything to do with the right to vote. Adults who don't have a job don't have the right to vote taken away.

Jason: Schools that are poor, which generally have more students that are going to fail, will have less of a say in the government than rich schools that are passing more kids. That becomes unfair and puts kids in a situation where those that are less well-off will have less of a voice. That's not at all how it should work. If anything, it should be the other way around.

CPL: If you had the ability to vote, would you vote Democrat or Republican?

Kehlen: That's a difficult question. We don't want this to turn into a party issue. It really affects everybody. It doesn't matter if you're Republican or Democrat.

3

The Voting Age Should Not Be Lowered

Philip Hensher

Philip Hensher is an English novelist and critic.

Proposals to lower the voting age are difficult to take seriously. Countries like North Korea and Sudan have lowered the voting age, but these countries are non-democratic. Lowering the voting age, then, is seldom connected to democratic freedoms. Furthermore, sixteen-year olds are simply too irresponsible to vote. Unlike adults, they have few social obligations (children, jobs), and because of their young age, no sense of history. Young voters would likewise be handicapped by excessive idealism. In their youthful zeal, young voters would make decisions that even they would regret in ten years' time.

At first, I thought this must be a joke. Or, since it was not quite that, perhaps a piece of blue-skies thinking emanating from some policy wonk who had started to wonder out loud without too much contemplation. Somehow, a silly idea had been floated in the think-tank on a quiet Friday morning, and before anyone could dismiss it, the idea had got into the newspapers where it would die a noisy death.

But apparently not. Lord Falconer, as Secretary of State for Constitutional Affairs, revealed that the Electoral Commission is conducting an inquiry into the voting age. Should people be given the vote at 16, rather than, as at present, as in all Britain's

Philip Hensher, "Politics Does Not Require an Influx of Idealism," *The Independent*, December 11, 2003. Copyright © 2007 Independent News and Media Limited. Reproduced by permission.

European partners, at 18? Lord Falconer said the Government was concerned about the lack of participation of young people in politics, and suggested that lowering the voting age might address this. Furthermore, he also raised the possibility that the lower age limit at which someone can become a Member of Parliament might be lowered from 21 to 18. All this is being presented with the utmost seriousness.

The first thing to say is that lowering the voting age would not place Britain in the vanguard of countries valuing democratic freedoms. Of the countries in the world which have a lower voting age than 18, North Korea, Indonesia and the Sudan set it at 17; Brazil, Cuba and Nicaragua at 16. Iran is apparently at the forefront of democratic liberalisation, with the age of suffrage there at 15 [Iran raised the voting age to 18 in January 2007.]. Quite consistently, the countries which have first lowered the voting age have been ruled by actively anti-democratic regimes. The first countries to lower the voting age to 18 were the Soviet Union and South Africa under apartheid. Conversely, within living memory, such otherwise exemplary democratic systems as Denmark and the Netherlands had a minimum voting age of 25.

Sixteen-year-olds, overwhelmingly, are irresponsible.

What does this curious fact suggest? Of course, there is no reason whatever why such countries as North Korea, the former Soviet Union or Iran should not have a voting age of 17, 15, or even 5—it would hardly make any difference when there is no democratic choice. It does show, however, that there is no necessary link between the widening of the franchise and democratic freedoms; indeed, there may be some reason to suspect that this move, in some circumstances, such as South African apartheid, may be used in an attempt to stifle dissent. In any circumstances, a party which lowers the voting age by two years would significantly alter the ideological flavour of the electorate. It would have the effect of adding a major city to the British electorate overnight; a population whose opinions and loyalty are quite different, in unpredictable ways, to the rest of the population.

Irresponsible and Idealistic Voters

Sixteen-year-olds, overwhelmingly, are irresponsible. I mean that in a non-pejorative sense; I mean that at that age, very few of them have had to take responsibility for anything, or have a practical understanding of responsibility. Few of them have children; a minority contributes directly to society, whether through taxation or any other means; few have a clear notion of what their lives will consist of, and only a hazy notion of the choices of politics.

Of course, much the same could be said of a great number of adults, and we don't object to adults voting for frivolous reasons, because they don't work or don't put anything back into society. But I do think there's a difference. There aren't many adults who don't have a sense, however vague, of responsibility; of how politics has impacted on their lives, and might do so in the future. Moreover, the whole point of judgement is experience. Even the most obtuse adult voter will have a sense of how this government compares with previous governments. Formative political experiences of my generation, say, might include the power cuts under the Heath government, the catastrophic events of Callaghan's administration, the miners' strike, and the vainglory and corruption of the Major years. [Heath, Callaghan, and Major were Prime Ministers]

The likely problem with lowering the voting age, almost certainly, is an influx of idealism.

Those sort of things, which everyone at the time noticed, don't necessarily mean that an older voter is a better voter, but certainly experience teaches a voter what can and cannot be achieved by politicians, and a sense of comparison. What are we going to do with a 16-year-old voter in 2005, who has no memory whatever of any administration before [former Prime Minister Tony] Blair's, since he was born in 1989? The answer, in practice, is that you tell them a lot of fairy stories about how evil the Tories were, and there is no reason why they shouldn't believe anything you said.

The likely problem with lowering the voting age, almost certainly, is an influx of idealism. Talking to young people about politics, what is immediately striking is an attitude of idealism about any given issue. That may not sound like a bad thing, but the positions which many, even most, young people cling to on, say, the environment, wealth distribution, or Iraq are simply not practical ones. Huge numbers of young people turned out to demonstrate against the war in Iraq, and it is fair to say that it is probably the dominant attitude among people in the 16–21 age group. But what did they actually want to be done? Even if you agree that it was unjustified to invade Iraq in the first place, what is to be done now? The predominant viewpoint in this age group shows exactly its fundamental irresponsibility, or, if you prefer, idealism, and it would be frankly dangerous to extend the franchise in this direction.

So why is the Government considering this move? They claim that it might extend democratic participation, and assume, surely correctly, that a democratic voice should not be linked to taxpaying or property-owning. But if that were an absolute good, why not extend the franchise to 10-year-olds, who similarly have views on public issues? Why have a minimum voting age at all?

Still more dangerous is the proposal that the minimum age of Members of Parliament be extended downwards to 18. It is not so much a practical danger, since no sane political party would put up an 18-year-old if there were any likelihood of the seat being won, nor is it easy to conceive of an 18-year-old with enough experience of the world to contribute usefully to parliamentary debate. The danger lies more in the attitude that the interests of young people can only be represented by one of their own; an attitude which could only result in their interests being neglected, as they were handed over to inexperienced and marginal spokesmen. In this case, the grown-ups probably know best.

What everyone should be concerned about is the possibility that extending the franchise will benefit one party at the expense of others. That, basically, would amount to gerrymandering, and the commission should be extremely wary of it. The likely result of an extension of the franchise will be, I guess, to strengthen the voice of extremist and impractical political agendas, although perhaps not to a damaging degree.

More seriously, the voice of the property-owning classes, of people trying to make money, of entrepreneurs and capitalists will not be reinforced to any appreciable degree. Some people might think it a good thing if idealistic socialism is given a boost at the expense of the Conservative Party. The point, however, is that if this were to come to pass, it should come about democratically, by reasoned debate in the adult electorate; and not, under any circumstances, by conscripting a large number of voters who, by definition, don't know what they are talking about and who, 10-years down the line, will for the most part realise the fact.

4

The Voting Age Should Be Eliminated

Association of Children's Suffrage

Association of Children's Suffrage is a student organization at Brown University committed to lowering the voting age.

As a member of a state/country, children, no matter what their age, should be allowed to vote. While many young voters may copy their parents voting patterns, this is hardly cause for concern: many youth share their parents' values. While critics fear that parents may force a child to vote prematurely or that politicians will attempt to win children's votes with tricks (free ice-cream), these concerns are over inflated. Also, voting rights will not automatically lead to other youth rights (like driver's licenses for six-year-olds). Everyone should care about children's suffrage. By denying youth the right to vote or "have a say" in civic affairs, adults are discounting their opinions, and not allowing youth a voice in laws (like curfews) that affect them. While extending the vote to children may seem unconventional, it is the next step in the ongoing expansion of suffrage rights.

W*hat does suffrage mean?*

Suffrage (súf·rij)—n. The right or privilege of voting as a member of a body, state, etc. (*Oxford English Dictionary*).

"Ten Questions, One Easy Answer," promotional material of the *Association of Children's Suffrage*, May 8, 2007. www.brown.edu/Students/Association_for_Childrens_Suffrage. Reproduced by permission of the Association for Children's Suffrage, founded 1997 at Brown University, Providence, RI.

In terms of the voting age, how low do you want to go?

All the way! We believe it's unfair to systematically reject citizens for trying to advance their own opinions. We therefore call for a simple universal criteria for voting: citizenship and sufficient interest to register and then vote on election day.

You want two-year-olds to vote?

We want two-year olds to *be able* to vote. Political interest grows with time, at different rates for different people. The majority of those who would vote if they could would most likely be in high school. After all, how many political two-year-olds have you met?

Won't child voters merely copy their parents?

Not all but, yes, most children would vote like their parents, as adults do. A well-regarded study of English voters in the 1980s reported that 90% of the Conservative party consisted of members whose parents both voted Conservative. Liberals were no different. Politically-mixed marriages sired politically mixed voters, half Liberal, half Conservative. Thus parents clearly influence children, but why at the expense of their individuality? Children's ideas belong no less to themselves when shared by others, including parents. Indeed, it makes sense that the family's interests are often common. A politician planning to build a road through a household of six deserves six less votes, not two. What's important is that children *could*, aware of their right to secret ballot, vote independently of parents; yet it should neither surprise nor disappoint anyone if many don't.

Political interest grows with time, at different rates for different people.

What about parents who force their children to vote prematurely?

A few parents, unusually unscrupulous, will always abuse their power. Of them, those who are unusually political might well commit voting fraud by forcing children to vote against their will. Similar fears of husbands manipulating their wives in the case of women's suffrage proved overinflated; that the majority of parents don't even vote suggests the same in the case of children's suffrage. Even so, lawbreakers should never hostage legislation, including a voting-age repeal. Abusive parents call for reform, not surrender.

Will politicians try and trick child voters with promises of free ice-cream, Disneyland, etc.?

Let them try. If such politicians convince a majority of mostly adults, they win with their condescending attitude of the young. But beware: though pork-barrel politics is not unknown to grown-ups, children may not prove as stupid as the patronizing think!

There is no reason why the extension of voting rights should automatically topple the legal structure guarding children.

What about the driving age, the draft age, the working age, statutory rape, limited right to contract, juvenile courts, compulsory school? Do you want to repeal some of these important laws protecting children?

Not necessarily. There is no reason why the extension of voting rights should automatically topple the legal structure guarding children. Thinking of voting rights like driving rights, for example, confuses the players for the score. Children might influence a lower driving age by voting, but only if their numbers and unanimity allowed. As long as most people agree that eight-year-olds threaten the roads (even most children would), eight-year-olds won't drive, regardless of their right to vote.

Why should I care about children's suffrage?

Citizenship counts. Yet 52% of voters in last year's elections preferred not to, proving that exclusion learned early lasts long. Citizenship without votes is like reading without books. Teachers could talk about it a lot, even hold simulations, but eighteen years later reading would seem distant and difficult—something for somebody else. Unfortunately, denying children's interest in political participation does more than hurt their civil education. It sends the message that their any idea is unworthy. Alienation, cynicism, even bigotry logically follow on the heels of discrimination. Children's suffrage offers the key benefit of a more civil citizenry: more involved, informed, vocal, diverse, and tolerant.

Why else should I care about children's suffrage?

Government affects children, so children should affect government. Consider the curfew laws, endorsed in 1996 by President Clinton and enforced in over 72% of major cities nationwide. Police arrest and fine children outside of their home during certain hours of the day, varying according to the city. That legislators denied those placed under a form of martial law the opportunity to elect their legislators violates the most basic protections of representative government, regardless of ones opinion on curfew laws themselves. Indeed, government probably impacts children most: it penalizes their transgressions, taxes their transactions, schedules their days in school, and takes over when their parents can't. Burdens of the future, such as debt, pollution, and social unrest, fall heaviest on children. There's room for improvement: currently, the debt exceeds $5 trillion, global temperature rises, and children make up the country's most impoverished, under-insured social group. Thus children stand ideally positioned to provide feedback. Their suffrage may well lead to better legislation.

The arguments make sense, but something still feels wrong about kids voting. Why?

Children's suffrage is unconventional. Indeed, never in history have children voted in government; most people haven't even considered the idea. Yet universal opportunity to political representation follows a historical trend started in ancient

Greece, formalized by Enlightenment philosophers, and extended in the United States by the Revolution and later suffrage movements of the propertyless, blacks, and women—all themselves radical in their times. Give children's suffrage time; it too will come.

5

Lowering the Voting Age Will Not Increase Voter Turnout

Votes for Adults

Votes for Adults is an organization dedicated to arguing against allowing 16-year-olds the right to vote.

While many believe that lowering the voting age will decrease voter turnout, the organization Votes At 16 argues that by allowing 16-year-olds the right to vote, they will form the habit of voting and vote more frequently. The argument's conclusion, however, has been based on faulty data, derived from an internet survey. It is difficult for voters to accurately recall their choices for short periods of time, much less six years previous. As a result, the representative figures of the internet survey were inflated, underlining a difference in voting behavior where none existed. As with Votes At 16's other arguments, the argument that lowering the voting age will increase voter turnout is confused.

In *How old is old enough?* the Electoral Commission states that its interest in the issue of age of electoral majority stems 'principally from our concern about declining participation rates in UK elections, especially among young people'.

It is all but universally accepted [however] that allowing 16 and 17-year olds to vote will have the result of *lowering* turnout in elections. Younger voters have always had lower turnout rates than older voters—for very obvious and perhaps understandable reasons—and lowering the age of electoral

Votes for Adults, "Why Voting Early Won't Mean Voting Often: Killing the 'Killer' Argument," May 9, 2007. http://votesforadults.typepad.com. Reproduced by permission.

majority will therefore simply lower overall turnout yet further. Even if 16 and 17 year olds would have a slightly higher propensity to vote than those aged 18–24 (as some proponents of the suggested change claim, on the basis of some very limited experiments in Germany), they would still be almost certain to be less likely to vote than the rest of the population. Even 'Votes At 16' has accepted that if the voting age is lowered then turnout in the next election will be lower than it would otherwise be. It is hard to see, then, how lowering the voting age would help to counter declining participation rates in UK elections.

Accordingly, advocates of a lower voting age have now begun to focus on a slightly different argument—a variant of the old adage 'vote early, vote often'. They claim that polling evidence shows that voters who attain voting age shortly before an election are more likely to vote than those who have to wait a few years for an election to come round. For example, in an article in the *New Statesman* (4 November 2002), [Member of Parliament] Nigel Griffiths and Beth Egan [Deputy Director of the Social Market Foundation] claimed the following:

> New polling . . . shows a link between the age at which people are finally able to vote in a general election and their inclination to use that vote thereafter. People who turn 18 in the year leading up to a general election are significantly more likely to bother to vote than those who turned 18 in the year after the previous general election and have therefore had to wait up to five years to get their hands on the stubby pencil tied to a bit of string.

> A turnout of only 49% was recorded in the 2001 election amongst the then 27 year olds who were 17 in 1992 and therefore had to wait until 1997 when they could finally vote in a general election at the age of 23. Amongst those who had just turned 18 in 1992, 65% bothered to vote in

2001. How many other simple factors can be shown to affect turnout by such a large [margin]?

This 'birth effect' cannot be put down to a mysterious accident in 1992 as similar findings hold for last year's election. In 2001 the oldest first-time voters at 22 had a turnout 14% lower than those voting within a year of turning 18.

These poll results are now widely used by 'Votes At 16' in its campaigning literature as one of its six reasons for lowering the voting age. They call it the 'birthday lottery'. Griffiths and Egan describe this as 'the killer argument for lowering the voting age', one 'which must be answered by all those who bemoan declining turnout and voter apathy', concluding: 'If it is true that those who vote young vote often then the case against lowering the voting age to 16, which has long been weak, is now indefensible'.

Misleading Polling Data

In fact, it is a sign of how weak the case for lowering the age of voting to 16 is that something this facile should be considered to be a 'killer argument' (or even an argument at all). There are very good reasons to dispute the validity of the poll results. Moreover, even if they were accepted, there is no logic behind the argument that such figures imply that the age of electoral majority should be lowered. . . .

The poll from which the data are derived was an internet poll undertaken by YouGov. It is worth noting that serious objections have been raised to internet polling by professionals in the industry—in particular when it extends beyond investigating simple voting intentions in current elections. . . Moreover, as the Commission should know, asking people to recall their votes is always a problematic exercise. There is a large literature showing that people have difficulty in remembering whether or not they voted even a couple of months after the election in question and that voting is always overreported. Yet here, the argument is based on respondents remembering whether they voted in elections held up to six years previously. Anyone with any experience of investigating turnout using survey data will know that figures based on recall over such a lengthy period are hardly worth reporting.

Given this it is little wonder that the turnout figures reported in this poll are frankly incredible. To ask us to believe that 19 year olds in 2001 had a turnout rate of 68 per cent (or even that 54 per cent of 22 year olds voted) beggars belief. Most other estimates put the figures for first-time voters somewhere in the 30s. Similarly, expecting us to believe that of those aged 23 in 1997 (that is, 17 year olds in 1992) 64 per cent voted, or 70 per cent of those aged 24, is stretching credulity. If these figures were anything like half accurate, then the UK would have had dramatically higher turnout in each of the last two elections—and we would not be engaging in this constant chest beating about supposed voter disengagement. Perhaps more pertinently, there would be no sign of any disengagement amongst young voters at all. In fact, of course, these data are so unreliable as to be meaningless.

The length of time that one has to wait before voting does not appear to have a consistent effect on the likelihood that one will vote in the future.

Moreover, anyone looking at the full data, rather than at the partial selection quoted by advocates of votes at 16, would soon come to the conclusion that there is no consistent 'vote early, vote often' effect anyway.

Based on exactly the same data set as used for Table 1, Table 2 shows the declared turnout rates of those who voted in 2001, broken down by their age in 1997. Unlike the situation shown in Table 1, there is no 'birthday lottery' effect at all. Those who had to wait the longest to vote in 2001—those who were 17 years old in 1997—were just two percentage points less likely to vote than those (aged 18) who had also been able to vote in 1997. Given the relatively small sample size involved (the overall survey had 1044 respondents, but covered all ages from 20 to 30, and so comparison of respondents of any two ages involves under 200 people), this is effectively no difference at all.

Table 2: Turnout in 2001, by age in 1997

Age in 1997	Turnout in 2001 (%)
17	65
18	67

One of the most striking features about the campaign for votes at 16 is how confused most of the arguments put forward by its proponents are.

Similarly, when you look at the full figures for first time voters in 2001—rather than merely the selective cases cited in Table 1—the birthday lottery looks noticeably less dramatic. Table 3 shows the figures for the turnout of first time voters in 2001, broken down by their age as in Table 1, but this time showing all the ages between 19 and 22. Whereas Table 1 showed a dramatic fall off from 68 per cent for those 19-year-old voters who got to vote straight away, down to 54 per cent for those who had to wait the longest, Table 3 shows a much less obvious trend. For most respondents there is almost no difference (and certainly no statistically significant difference) between the turnout rates of first-time voters depending on how long they have to wait to exercise their vote. The figures for 19-, 20- and 21-year-old voters are almost identical. Those who have to wait the very longest do appear to be the least likely to vote, but the constant nature of the figures for the other three ages makes this look much more like a blip than when the data are displayed without the middle two age categories shown.

Table 3: Turnout of first time voter in 2001, by age

Age of first-time voter in 2001	Turnout (%)
22	54
21	67
20	65
19	68

Killing the "Killer" Argument

A proper analysis of data therefore does not reveal any general 'birthday lottery' effect. The length of time that one has to wait before first voting does not appear to have a consistent effect on the likelihood that one will vote in the future. Rather the differences are sporadic and/or so marginal as to be meaningless.

But even if one chooses to accept these data as reliable (even when they are clearly not), and their interpretation as accurate (even when it is clearly not) it is worth thinking about what it is being claimed. The final argument against the vote early, vote often claim—the killer argument, if you will—is that it is frankly irrelevant to the question of votes at 16. It merely shows that anyone aged 18 in an election year will be more likely to vote in future elections than those who have had to wait a year or two. But so what? This effect—if that is what it is—would presumably apply whatever the age of electoral majority. If the voting age is lowered to 16, then those aged 15 in an election year will be less likely to vote in future elections than those aged 16. Lower the age to 14 and it'd be 13 year olds that would be affected. The effect cannot, therefore, in itself be an argument for lowering the voting age.

One of the most striking features about the campaign for votes at 16 is how confused most of the arguments put forward by its proponents are. Most of the arguments about equalisation—why can a 16 year old have sex, but not vote?—are simply feeble. Arguments about no taxation without representation founder both on the low percentage of 16-year-olds who actually pay income tax and on the high percentage of children who pay VAT.

The arguments to which the Electoral Commission should attach most weight—given its remit—should be the effect that the change would have on turnout. Almost everyone accepts that enfranchising 16–17 year olds will lower turnout in the short-term. Proponents of change are therefore forced to claim that turnout will be higher in the long run because the younger people are when they first vote, the more likely they are to do so in the future.

Yet as has been demonstrated this claim is based on very dubious evidence and even more dubious logic. In these ways it is similar to most of the other arguments for votes at 16.

6

Lowering the Voting Age Will Increase Voter Turnout

Keith Mandell

Keith Mandell is the Chapter Formation Director of Youth Rights Association.

Apathy is a major problem with the American voter, and lowering the voting age is one way to encourage political involvement. The organization Kids Voting has even shown that when young Americans are allowed to take part in elections, even their parents vote more frequently. The connection between children's involvement and adult participation is strongest among families from lower socio-economic backgrounds, the class of citizens with the lowest voter participation. Participation in Kids Voting has also shown that contrary to popular belief, many children are interested in politics. Early participation will help young Americans form an interest in politics before they have a chance to become apathetic.

Apathy among voters today is a major problem in American democracy. In the 1998 elections, only 36.1% of the voting age population turned out to vote, the lowest percentage since 1942, when America was at war. Even in a presidential election year, 1996, turnout was only 49%. This level of turnout makes building a thriving democracy difficult.

Many nonvoters express a lack of confidence in our democratic system. They hold strong positions on issues, but do not

Keith Mandell, "A Proposal to Lower the Voting Age," *National Youth Rights Association—Voting Age Research,* www.youthrights.org/voteproposal.php. Reproduced by permission of the author.

believe government cares about them or their problems. Ironically, low voter turnout sends government a message that nonvoters do not care about politics, leading to important issues being ignored. This neglect must stop.

Lowering the voting age to sixteen can be a small but meaningful step in raising voter turnout in the District [District of Columbia]. How can this be done? A lower voting age, combined with a curriculum designed to teach young people about the political process can increase their interest in voting. This increased interest will be passed on to their parents through after-school and dinner table conversations. Nonvoting parents will be encouraged by their children's enthusiasm to vote.

This theory has been tested and proven successful in the case of the Kids Voting, a national mock election program which allows children in grades K-12 to vote at the polls while learning about the political process through a comprehensive classroom curriculum.

Increasing Voter Turnout

Kids Voting has had extremely positive results. Not only were young people enthusiastic about politics, but some of that enthusiasm rubbed off onto their parents. The result was a higher turnout among adults.

A 1996 survey by Bruce Merrill, an Arizona State University journalism professor, found a strong increase in turnout. Merrill compared turnout of registered voters in five cities with Kids Voting with turnout in five cities without the program. Merrill found that between five and ten percent of respondents reported Kids Voting was a factor in their decision to vote. This indicated that 600,000 adults nationwide were encouraged to vote by the program. Turnout increases in individual districts were even more impressive. In Erie County, New York, one-third of all adults considered Kids Voting an important factor in bringing them to the polls. For eleven percent it was the determining factor.

A 1994 survey by Merrill showed a smaller overall increase in voting, but very impressive increases in particular states. Merrill found that among fifteen states surveyed, fourteen had higher turnouts. Washington State boasted an increased turnout of 9%, while Georgia, Tennessee, South Carolina and Kansas all had more than 5% increases as a result of the Kids Voting program. An earlier study in Arizona by Merrill found that Kids Voting had a cumulative effect: School districts that used the program in two election cycles had higher turnouts than those that only used it in one.

Few studies have measured the effect of Kids Voting in the District of Columbia. The program existed here from 1994 until 1996 and appears to have had positive effects. The District's voter turnout in 1996 (40.9%) was higher than it had averaged during the period 1972–1988, before Kid Voting became part of the curriculum (36.32%). Admittedly some of that increase may have been due to "motor voter" legislation enacted in 1992. However, that four percentage point increase was far higher than the seven other states which also enacted motor voting laws in 1992, suggesting Kids Voting played a prominent role in increasing voter turnout.

Active participation in the political process will lead to a lifetime of voting.

How did letting young people vote encourage turnout among their parents? A study by Stephen Chafee of Stanford University found that increased political discussions between parents and children were the major factor in increasing turnout. Chafee surveyed 457 students in San Jose, California, along with one parent of each student. One half of the students surveyed had participated in the Kids Voting program.

Chafee found that there was a strong correlation (.43) between exposure of students to Kids Voting and discussions about politics between parents and children. Parents of Kids Voting children were far more likely to discuss politics with their children than those whose children had not been part of the program.

Chafee found that the effects of Kids Voting were strongest among parents of children in lower socio-economic backgrounds. The correlation between exposure to the Kids Voting program and increased political discussions between parents and children was greater (.49) among parents from low income groups than it was among wealthier parents (.33). This suggests that poorer parents, who are least likely to vote would be encouraged to vote by the enthusiasm of their children. Finally, Chafee found almost no correlation between exposure to Kids Voting and parents initiating political discussions with their children (.08). This means that the young people themselves were starting these discussions, which encouraged their parents to get out and vote.

Chafee also found a correlation between the Kids Voting program, and increased knowledge among adults of candidates' backgrounds (.22 correlation), and an increased active reflection of the news (.15 correlation). Again there was a much greater correlation among lower income parents (.37 and .26 respectively).

The fact that Kids Voting has its greatest impact among parents of children from lower socio-economic backgrounds is especially important for the District of Columbia. About 63% of District students receive free lunches, which require students come from lower income backgrounds. The Kids Voting curriculum in Washington DC appears to have had a positive impact on voter turnout in the District. If the program is brought back, such effects would most likely occur again. . . .

A Lifetime of Voting

In addition to adults, youth would benefit by a lower voting age. Young people want to vote and would turn out in high numbers. Active participation in the political process will lead to a lifetime of voting.

In order for young people to benefit from a lower voting age, they must first show interest in elections and politics. Poll after poll suggests young people want the right to vote. This interest begins early in childhood and continues into high school. In 1992, Sesame Place, a children's amusement park in the Philadelphia area, conducted a survey of young people aged eight to twelve. It found that 89% wanted the right to vote. Among teens, this interest in voting persists. A 1991 poll taken at a mock election in Minneapolis, Minnesota found that 73% of teens 12–17 supported a voting age of sixteen. Young people are ready and willing to vote, if given the chance.

Young people also have a strong interest in politics generally, despite the conventional wisdom that they are much more concerned with other matters. A 1992 survey of 12–17 year olds conducted for the *Washington Post* found that 73% were very interested or fairly interested in politics, while only 27% were not very interested or not at all interested. About 95% of these young people viewed voting in a presidential election as very important or fairly important.

In order for a lower voting age to succeed, young people would also have to turn out in large numbers to vote. Available evidence from the U.S. and abroad suggests they would do so.

In Germany in 1996, several German states lowered their voting age to sixteen for local elections. The results were impressive. In Lower Saxony's capital city of Hanover sixteen and seventeen year olds turned out at a higher rate (56.5%) than did 18–24 year olds (49%). In the state of Bransscheig, male voters under eighteen turned out at a 52.5% clip, besting turnout for male voters aged 18–45. Likewise 16–18 year old female voters turned out at a higher rate (48.5%) than females 18–25 (42.6%). In 1999, the state of Sachsen Anhalt lowered its voting age, with similar results. In the city of Kreisfreie, under eighteen voters turned out at a higher rate than voters aged 18–30.

Austria experienced a similar youth voting boom after several of its states reduced the voting age to sixteen for local elections. Voter turnout among sixteen and seventeen year-olds approached or exceeded not just that of young adults (with their notoriously low turnout) but of the adult population as a whole. In a 2002 Burgenland election, sixteen- and seventeen-year-olds turned out at 81%, only 5% lower than the entire adult population. [Source: "Wahlect am 16" "Right to Vote [at] 16" http://www.lars-tietjen.de/download/beteiligung.pdf.] In Vienna's 2005 election, under-eighteen turnout (59%) virtually equaled adult turnout. [Source: Veronkia Oleksyn, "Austrians Split on Lower Voting Age," Associated Press Article, January 12, 2007.] Finally, in 2003, youth in the city of Graz turned out at a higher rate (58%) than the population as a whole (57%). [Source: Local Governments in Austria, "The Politico-Administrative System and New Developments since the 1990's," Diputacio Barcelona xarxa de municipis, at 52.] Following this impressive turnout of young voters in local elections, in 2007 Austria became the first European Union nation to lower its national voting age to sixteen. [Source: "Austrian Parliament Passes Law Lowering Voting Age to 16," Associated Press Article, June 5, 2007.]

In the United States, no state or locality has set a voting age lower than eighteen. We must examine evidence from Kids Voting and other mock election sources to determine what turnout might be for young people, as well as the additional benefits of youth political participation.

Kids Voting USA has been a huge success at getting young people to vote. In 1996, almost five million cast ballots in local, state and national elections. While five million is only a fraction of the number of people aged 5–17, Kids Voting USA only reached 40 states in 1996. In many of these states, only a few school districts operated the program.

"Kids Voting" Suggests Political Interest

The Kids Voting organization does not keep data on what percentage of students in Kids Voting districts actually voted. It is possible, however, to evaluate Kids Voting turnout based on information from particular districts. In 1994, in the District of Columbia, more than half of all eligible students cast ballots. This is especially impressive in an off-year election in which 40% of District adults voted. In 1996, Lee's Summit, Missouri saw 7,000 students turn out to vote, almost 60 percent of its student population. In 1996, in Wake County, North Carolina, 43,000 students turned out to vote when only 30,000 had been expected, causing polling places to run out of ballots. In 1998 mid-term elections, truly impressive turnout was seen in Shawnee County, Kansas. Among students, 78% turned out to vote. This is especially high considering some children under fourteen were kept from voting by nonvoting parents. Young people were determined to cast their ballots, and did so in enormous numbers.

A voting age of sixteen can introduce young people to the political process before they become apathetic.

One more indication of young people's interest in voting can be seen in Minneapolis, Minnesota. In 1991, the school district allowed young people to cast mock ballots at polling places for a school board election. While only 5.6% of adults showed up at the polls, 40% of teens aged 12–17 turned out to make their voices heard.

Kids Voting students gain a great deal of political knowledge as well as enthusiasm for the process. Stephen Chafee's study found that San Jose Kids Voting participants were more likely to have political discussions with parents or friends (.50 and .41 correlation respectively), than non-participants. Again, as found in the survey of parents, these correlations were more pronounced among children in the lower socio-economic strata (.54 and .49 correlation respectively). Thus the impact in Washington will be greatest among the District's many low-income students.

Another survey, Bruce Merrill's study of Kids Voting from the 1994 election, further reveals student enthusiasm for the program. Merrill surveyed a total of 24,572 participants. Almost 70% wanted Kids Voting to be brought back to their school for the next election, while only 11% preferred the program not return. The remaining students were undecided.

Merrill's survey also shows the extent to which the Kids Voting program helped young people gain political awareness. More than 71% of students reported frequently or occasionally questioning parents about elections at home. These same students also viewed voting with great importance. About 94% felt it was very important or somewhat important to vote.

How can a lower voting age stop voter apathy among young adults and lead to lifetime electoral participation? It can be done through the meaningful involvement of youth in elections. Young people want to be a part of the process, but are too often told their opinion does not matter. By the time many reach college, they are cynical of the political system. A voting age of sixteen can introduce young people to the political process before they become apathetic.

The lesson learned from Kids Voting in the District and elsewhere is clear: Young people will become energized about elections in which they actively participate rather than a merely observe. Young people want government to listen to them. A lower voting age will do more than just increase youth interest in politics; it will provide a forum to encourage government to address the concerns of youth.

7

Lowering the Voting Age Will Protect Youth Interests

Duncan Lindsey

Duncan Lindsey is a Professor of Social Welfare at UCLA.

Although the United States is a wealthy country, millions of children continue to live in poverty. And while organizations like the Children's Defense Fund believe that eliminating children's poverty is a realistic goal, few politicians have pursued this goal. Why hasn't the problem been addressed? For the simple reason that children are disenfranchised. Without possessing a vote, there is little chance of children (or any other group) gaining the attention of elected officials. Enfranchising children may not immediately solve the problem of poverty, but it will provide children with a foundation for political representation. This in itself "will add to the political and moral wealth of the nation."

The largest category of poor in the United States are children. There are more than 14 and a half million children in the United States who live in poverty, while more than 5 million children live in families with less than half the poverty line income. Too young to carry their own cause, these children often suffer out of the limelight and in silence. These figures seem implausible in a nation of such enormous wealth.

Why have we allowed such poverty to persist among such a precious resource as our children? It certainly isn't because we don't know what to do. Child welfare policies and programs that could end child poverty have been available during

Duncan Lindsey, "Why Children Should Have a Vote," *Child Welfare*, May 14, 2007. Reproduced by permission.

the last several decades. This isn't rocket science. Nor is it the cost of these policies and programs which stops us. As the Children's Defense Fund has pointed out, we could end child poverty for less than three percent of all federal spending.

There is a collective will to end child poverty and support for the expenditure required, even in a time of massive federal government budget deficits. It isn't the money that stops us. What prevents us from ending child poverty? The fundamental problem is that our political system fails to provide a mechanism that lets the interests of children to be represented. In modern democratic societies like the United States, political power derives from the vote. Those who can vote are able to assure that their needs and interests are protected. Yet, children are unable to vote.

Voting Equals Political Power

One could imagine the consequences for any particular group if they lost their right to vote. Their interests would depend on the good will and sympathy of others. Perhaps their rights would be protected by the courts. But in very real terms, their interests and needs would rapidly fall in importance among elected officials.

Until children have representation in the democratic political system, their needs will be neglected.

One could imagine, for example, about what would happen to seniors, if a law was passed ending the right to vote for those over 65 years of age. It wouldn't take long for the Social Security System to be raided. Seniors would find Medicare and Medicaid being gutted. The condition for senior citizens would rapidly decline. In no time at all, seniors might find themselves in the same situation as children. Seniors would lose their political power and become dependent on the good will and sympathy of others who have their own compelling interests.

One in five children in North America live in poverty. The enormous wealth of these countries makes this fact almost incomprehensible. Nevertheless, children have seen their needs placed at the back of the national agenda. Several years ago all of the major political parties in Canada agreed to an idea called Canada 2000. Accordingly, the goal was to unite and work together in a non-partisan basis so that by the year 2000 poverty among children would be eliminated. To date, very little action has followed these words. The goal was a noble gesture that has failed to produce any real programs or policies. As with so many other pronouncements on behalf of children, they end up, over the long haul, to be empty promises. Too many other concerns surface that have more powerful voting blocks and constituencies behind them. Lacking political power, the concerns of children are set to the side. If we ever hope to end widespread poverty among children, then we need to think about ways to insure that the interests and needs of children are represented. We need to think what, until now, has been unthinkable.

If children were given the franchise, then their interests and needs would receive attention equal to other groups in democratic society.

Until children have representation in the democratic political system, their needs will be neglected. Progress toward gaining children the right to representation will take time. Efforts to lower the voting age will require a constitutional amendment in the United States. However, until we recognize the centrality of the child's right to vote, progress will be episodic and short lived.

Enfranchising Children

We need to consider giving children the right to vote at age 16 (or even 14 after they have developed the required formal thought processes) or the right to assign their proxy. Obviously before they develop the cognitive skills and emotional maturity necessary for making difficult political judgments, children cannot be expected to vote. Perhaps these children should have their right to vote exercised by proxy.

We could assign their proxy to their principal care giver. If children were given the franchise, then their interests and needs would receive attention equal to other groups in democratic society. To restore our obligation to children will require imaginative solutions that today seem unthinkable. It wasn't that many years ago when blacks were denied to right to vote. Women received the franchise with the 19th Amendment in 1920. Perhaps we can experiment with giving children the right to vote. Until children have the right to vote, we may simply continue a cycle of concern and neglect of children's issues that has failed to produce substantial progress.

It might be argued that providing women with the right to vote has not really led to fundamental changes or improvements for women. Unquestionably, progress for women has been too slow. But it would be hard to imagine what the situation of women would have been (or would become) without the right to vote. It would be unthinkable to even imagine a situation where women were denied the right to vote.

Government establishes the rules the community will abide by in deciding how resources (such as the Gross Domestic Product) will be distributed. In a society where special interest politics shape governmental interests, those groups able to fund the campaigns of elected officials will see their interests protected and legislation which is favorable to protecting and improving their interests enacted. Likewise, those groups who are unable to make substantial contributions to the campaigns of elected officials will see their interests go unprotected. Further, those groups, such as the poor, who have historically recorded low voter turnout will be especially vulnerable. And most of all, those who do not vote (i.e., children) are unlikely to have their interests protected and will likely fare poorly in competition with others in the arena of political decision-making.

We can lay the foundation for ending widespread poverty among children only by empowering the children themselves. This will require giving children the right to representation. The mechanism for achieving this representation will require creative and innovative problem solving, but we can do it. What we need to do is give up some of our own power so that children can have what we already enjoy. It won't cost us any money. It won't add to the federal deficit. But it will add to the political and moral wealth of the nation. We ought to be able to enter the next millennium with our children having equal representation in our political institutions.

8

Youth Are Too Self-Centered to Vote

Mary Beth Hicks

Mary Beth Hicks is a columnist for the Washington Times *and author of* The Perfect World Inside My Minivan.

The fact that some people believe that children should be allowed to vote insinuates that everyone votes for no better reason than self-interest. Children's votes, after all, would reflect selfish personal issues like being allowed to eat cookies for breakfast. And if children are allowed to vote, why not allow children to run for office? As with children's votes, a child candidate's campaign would be based on selfish issues like being allowed to skip school. While it may be a good idea for children to accompany adults to the polls in order to learn about the political process, only a child-centric culture would think that it was a good idea for children to vote.

"Mom, I have a question," my daughter says as she buckles her seat belt for the short ride to school. Usually when there's an introduction to the question, it's long and complicated. This one is short and complicated.

"What's the difference between Republicans and Democrats?"

Do I answer with a history lesson or a quick overview of the whole "red state, blue state" thing? I haven't had enough coffee for either reply, and besides, this is a topic my husband loves to address.

"Let's discuss that at dinner," I say, dodging the question.

I have spent the better part of a month driving my children about town while answering questions such as this about our political process. My children's curiosity is inspired by yard signs, billboards and radio ads, the combination of which have transformed my van into a mobile civics class.

Most of the time, I can come up with clear and concise explanations.

"What does gubernatorial mean?" (About the governor).

If children were permitted to vote, it seems only fair they also should be allowed to run for office.

"Why are the voices on radio ads usually women?" (Because women listen to the radio and the candidates want women to vote for them).

"Why does that candidate have pink yard signs?" (Some questions have no good answer.)

"Why can't kids vote?" (Because you have too many questions.)

Believe it or not, at least one child-welfare expert believes children's suffrage would be a good way to promote the well-being of our youngest citizens. This expert is a college professor, so of course his notion has something to do with the fair "distribution of resources."

Self Interest and Voting

The idea that children could participate meaningfully in the political process suggests that all it takes to be a voter is a simplistic sense of self-interest. I would like to think it requires more than that, but sadly, the professor may have a point. Hmmm.

If children were permitted to vote, it seems only fair they also should be allowed to run for office. After all, it wouldn't be a truly representative form of government if children couldn't cast their ballots for those whose interests and opinions about the role of government reflect their own.

If this were possible, I can easily see Amy, my 9-year-old, running for Congress. Her platform? Nutrition, freedom and personal responsibility.

Children should have Oreo cookies for breakfast—and not sneak them, but really be allowed to eat them in the family room in front of the TV. After they eat the cream filling out of the inside, children should be free to put the remaining unwanted cookies under the sofa cushion. When the cookies are discovered, children should not have to accept personal responsibility for the mess.

Children should go to school only on the days when they want to go. If they're too tired when the alarm clock goes off at 7 in the morning, they should be free to just skip school or go later when it's almost time for recess.

Children should not be required to do a lot of boring chores such as making the bed, loading or unloading the dishwasher or bringing baskets of dirty clothes to the laundry room. Someone else should take personal responsibility for those jobs, especially if heavy lifting is involved.

I think Amy would run a polished campaign. She would articulate her opinions on the issues, and like all modern-day politicians, if she were tripped up by a tough question she would stay "on message."

Maybe I'm a voting snob, but some people don't have what it takes to make well-reasoned choices. We call these people "children."

(Example: "Amy, isn't it lazy and irresponsible to make someone else carry your dirty clothes to the laundry room?" Amy: "If parents loved their children, they would buy them new clothes, such as the really cute leggings worn by Disney's 'Cheetah Girls.'")

All kidding aside, anyone who suggests that children should participate in our political process has never witnessed a student council election.

More important, he never has stayed up until after 10 on a school night helping to make posters for the important job of student body secretary.

Nor has he listened over and over to a campaign speech that highlights the candidate's organizational skills, typing speed and creative use of highlighter pens, only to scoop up that well-qualified candidate after school and hear about how the entire slate of popular girls won all the offices—even though they didn't bother to make posters.

A Child-Centric Culture

Maybe I'm a voting snob, but some people don't have what it takes to make well-reasoned choices. We call these people "children."

Of course, even if they can't actually vote, my children love coming along with me to the polls. This is a great way to show them what it means to exercise my civic duty of participation. It also eliminates the prospect of "hanging chads" because the younger ones always want a turn to punch the stylus through the ballot card.

Tagging along with mom or dad is a learning opportunity. In contrast, investing children with a right to vote strikes me as the kind of preposterous suggestion you make when you elevate children to a place of unwarranted social status. Children's suffrage would be yet another outrageous result of a child-centric culture.

We adults ought to vote, and when we do, we ought to make choices that reflect our ideas about what's best for our communities, our country and our world. I just can't imagine the Founding Fathers envisioned us voting for whatever we think would most benefit our own children.

Then again, even if that was my goal, I'd be foiled because last time I checked there was no Proposal O (r-e-o) on the ballot.

9

Adolescents Are Too Immature to Vote

Nicolas Kohler and Colin Campbell with Steve Maich

Nicolas Kohler and Colin Campbell write for Maclean's Magazine.

*Voter turnout has traditionally been lower for young adults in
the United States, Canada, and the United Kingdom. While
many have suggested that lowering the voting age to 16 will
raise turnout, new evidence has suggested that 16-year-olds—
and even 18-year-olds—may be too immature to vote. Since the
voting age was lowered in Canada (1970) and the United States
(1971), many hallmarks of youth—living at home, working, and
attending school—have been prolonged, essentially putting off
adulthood. Researchers have also suggested that the teenage
brain is insufficiently developed, especially pertaining to judg-
ment and impulse control. Young voters have shown little interest in the political process. Realizing that few young people vote,
few politicians are unwilling to address their concerns. While a
number of groups have worked to raise young adults' interest in
the political process, they have met with limited success. Lowering the voting age for a disinterested population is unlikely to resolve the dilemma.*

In the spring of 2004, a million Canadians received a letter
in the mail reminding them to vote in the upcoming sum-

Nicolas Kohler and Colin Campbell with Steve Maich, "Stop Him Before He Votes,"
Maclean's Magazine, January 16, 2006. Copyright © 2006 Rogers Publishing. Reproduced by permission.

mer election. All had turned 18 since 2000, when Jean Chrétien [Prime Minister] won his third consecutive majority, and
all had earned the right to cast a ballot. Few did. Despite the
mass-mailed exhortations by Canada's chief electoral officer,
Jean-Pierre Kingsley, just 38.7 per cent of Canadians between
the ages of 18 and 21 voted, adding to what Kingsley called a
"disturbing" trend among young people. "The decline in turnout at federal elections since 1988 is largely confined to those
Canadians born after 1970," he said in a speech.

Young people don't vote, a problem that's now discussed
so much that our eyes can be forgiven for glazing over—like a
teenager's in a civics class—whenever it's raised. In Canada,
the U.S., the U.K. and elsewhere, there are high-profile campaigns to try and lower the voting age to 16 in the hope it will
encourage young people to take part in the democratic process.

But there's a growing body of evidence to suggest that's a
wrong-headed approach. Scientific, sociological and demographic evidence indicates that young people are, in essence,
too immature and too detached from functioning society to
be entrusted with the vote. What if the move to lower the age
from 21 to 18 was wrong in the first place and ought to be re-
versed?

The idea of raising the age of suffrage isn't that far-fetched.
It was only in 1970, after all, that the federal government hit
upon 18 as a good age to start kids voting. But kids today
aren't what they were in 1970—not the stakeholders in the
political process, nor the models of civic engagement their
boomer parents once aspired to be. Many today still live at
home, more remain in school longer, and more move willy-
nilly from job to job before settling on a career. In 1971, 22
per cent of Canadians between 15 and 19 held full-time jobs,
compared with just 13 per cent in 2001, according to Statistics
Canada. "The traditional adulthood of duty and self-sacrifice
is becoming more and more a thing of the past," James Côté,

a sociologist at the University of Western Ontario, explains. In 1970, adolescence ended abruptly after the age of 19; now it languishes well into one's 20s or 30s.

Extended Adolescence

Putting adulthood off for so long means 18-year-olds have more in common with children than with the 30-year-olds with whom they share the vote. In the U.S., "18-year-olds are pretty incompetent," said Michael Barone, author of *Hard America, Soft America.* "You watch them at McDonald's and they don't know what to do. But American 30-year-olds are the most competent 30-year-olds in the world." In his book, Barone argues that young people under the age of 18 now live in what he calls "soft America," where they remain sheltered from the rigours of competition and accountability. After 18, at university, community colleges or in the private sector, they move into "hard America" and "develop the abilities of productivity, competence and creativity far above what most people at 18 thought they were capable of."

Young people today have essentially tuned out.

That shift in the social fabric—extending the security blanket of childhood into the mid-20s and beyond—is mirrored by new scientific research into the brain's development. Medical science is now awash in studies showing how teenage brains are underdeveloped, particularly in areas dealing with judgement and impulse control. For example, Deborah Yurgelun-Todd, a research scientist at Harvard Medical School, has found young people often have difficulty interpreting complex cues from the world around them. "Just because teens are physically mature, they may not appreciate the consequences or weigh information the same way as adults do," she told reporters in 2004. "Good judgement is learned, but you can't learn it if you don't have the necessary hardware."

Bolstering that opinion is a recent study by the U.S. National Institutes of Health, which found that brain functions controlling judgement and risk assessment—the human brain's so-called "executive branch"—aren't fully mature until age 25. Ruben Gur, a professor of psychology and director of the Brain Behavior Laboratory at the University of Pennsylvania, has found that the parts of the brain most important to critical thinking are the last to develop. Neurological science, Gur has said, argues for raising the age of legal majority to 22 or 23. Not surprisingly, much of this research has been used to advance arguments in some U.S. states that the age of sexual consent, as well as the legal age for smoking, drinking and driving a car should be raised. In Ontario and Michigan, efforts are being made to bring the age of mandatory school attendance to 18.

If there's nothing on the political menu appetizing to those between 18 and 21, there's even less incentive for them to vote.

Lower Voter Turnout

Put kids with half-baked brains in a North America that's learned to coddle its young and you get a group of voters who can't manage to scratch an X on a ballot. Since it dropped the voting age in 1970, Canada has watched its turnout rate drop. The move 35 years ago came amid a flurry of similar changes around the world driven largely by the politically active baby-boom generation. "At the time, Trudeau argued that this was to assuage the intergenerational conflict and the upsurge of youth activism," said Dennis Pilon, a Trent University political scientist. "He felt this was a move that would incorporate young people into the political system at a time they were challenging it and raising questions." Then-U.S. President Richard Nixon was a leading supporter of the change south of the border and gushed about the benefits of extending the franchise to 11 million new voters—many of them barely out of high school. "You will infuse into this nation some idealism, some courage, some stamina, some high moral purpose," Nixon said.

How wrong they were: though voter-turnout rates among Canadians of all ages had been in slow but steady decline for decades, they dropped steeply after 1988—the same year those born in 1970 reached 18 and earned the right to vote. The U.S., which lowered its voting age from 21 to 18 a year after Canada with the passage of the 26th Amendment, has witnessed a similar trend. Indeed, lowering the voting age didn't have the effect many expected—or hoped for. Young people today have essentially tuned out. According to one Elections Canada survey of Canadian youths immediately after the 2000 federal election, one in five could not name Jean Chrétien as leader of the Liberal Party and half could not identify former Prime Minister Joe Clark as leader of the Progressive Conservatives.

Notwithstanding Nixon's promise that 18-year-olds would deliver idealism, courage and stamina, North Americans have seen cynicism and apathy. The young have never swayed an election in Canada or the U.S., nor have political parties found it profitable to court them, preferring older voters who are more consistent and whose issues now dominate elections. What's developed is an almost unbreakable vicious cycle, argues Lawrence LeDuc, a University of Toronto political scientist who's done numerous studies on voting patterns. The young are the driving force behind the disturbing decline in voter turnout rates in the past 10 to 15 years. While those over 60 still vote at more or less the same rate as always (upwards of 80 per cent), only 25 per cent of young people cast ballots. "Each new younger group that comes in seems to vote at lower rates and over time it tends to pull the total turnout down," said LeDuc.

The pattern has distorted our politics: "It's why we have so many aging white-male politicians going around talking about health care and why it's hard to raise issues that are relevant to younger people," said LeDuc. If there's nothing on the political menu appetizing to those between 18 and 21, there's even less incentive for them to vote. And if youth don't vote, there's no incentive for politicians to cater to issues of concern to them.

Encouraging the Youth Vote

The current campaign hasn't changed this status quo. "This election, to be honest, if I could ignore it, I would," said Ilona Dougherty, the 25-year-old founder of Apathy is Boring, a non-profit group aimed at trying to bring young people back to the democratic process. Dougherty, who is not an advocate of changing the voting age, agrees politicians have failed to connect with young people. "I don't think we should just be encouraging youth with 'rah-rah, go vote, it's your civic duty.' We really need to look at fundamental systemic reasons why young people are not voting."

One hypothesis put forth, said Pilon, the Trent University political scientist, is that giving the vote to 18-year-olds introduces them to the process "when they are least anchored," either shuttling between home and university or caught in the transition between high school and the rest of their lives. "When the voting age was dropped to 18, you got a whole generation of people who didn't establish a very good relationship with the political system." Many, confronted with an election and feeling unprepared, ended up not voting at all. The precedent made it all the more likely they would not cast a ballot in the election after that, and the election after that— and so on.

In response, Elections Canada has sunk piles of money into encouraging the young to vote. Just as he did in the last election, Jean-Pierre Kingsley, the chief electoral officer, has sent 275,000 letters of encouragement to Canadians who have since turned 18. In addition to a television commercial with a rap-music theme, Elections Canada is advertising in movie theatres to capture the interest of young people. There will be 347 more polls on university campuses or near student ghettos to make voting easier. There's little evidence, however, that such programs work. "They'd like some of us academics to tell them that the things they are doing are going to resolve the problem—and we don't think so," said LeDuc. "The demographic drivers are just too strong."

Lowering the Voting Age

Some believe the answer lies in reducing the voting age even further. Mark Holland, the incumbent Liberal MP for Ajax-Pickering, introduced a private member's bill to reduce the age of suffrage to 16; the new voters would register in high school, thereby habituating them to the process. (The bill died over the summer.) Young people, Holland said, "don't know how to get on the voter's list, they don't know how much information they need to vote—they never really got that practical element." He added: "They're an incredibly hard group to find." While on the campaign trail, Holland seeks them out, "going to the mall, going to the local drinking establishments." While they're still in school, "We know where they are, we know how to register them," he said. "What do we have to lose in this? What's the worst thing that could happen?"

According to some—a lot. "Reducing the voting age to 16 would be a dreadful mistake," said David Denver, a professor of politics at Lancaster University, in Britain, where a well-developed movement to lower the voting age also exists. "What is the political memory of a 16-year-old?" said Denver, who has written several articles and studies opposing the idea. "My university students can't remember Mrs. Thatcher, they can't really remember anything before Blair," he said. "If you let a 16-year-old vote, they wouldn't even remember an entire government term. They simply have no basis on which to make any kind of judgement." Young people have never been interested in voting, he argued: "What are young people interested in? Sex, drink, clubs—enjoying themselves."

Then Denver goes a step further. "One might argue that if you were to put the voting age back up again—to 21—you'd make the vote more valuable," he said. "People might realize that the vote isn't just something cheap, to be dished out to kids. People might take it more seriously." Voter turnout, he added, is declining in part because most mainstream parties have crowded into the centre of the political spectrum. All of them, like carnival barkers jostling for rubes, yell out much the same pitch, one honed through years of appealing to older voters.

Were Canada to raise the voting age to 21, the young would not be disenfranchised but rather would be given back their teeth. Older voters could keep their dentures and their political concerns about hospital waiting times and the latest bean-counting scandal—all lost on the young. Political parties, meanwhile, would be forced to contend with something new: a sector of the population that has not learned how not to vote from the tender age of 18—but who can cast a ballot that means something.

10

Youth Enfranchisement Is a Moral Necessity

Leo Semashko

Leo Semashko is the director of the Public Institute of Strategic Sphere Studies in St. Petersburg, Russia.

The right to vote has grown extensively in democracies since the industrial era, but an important group remains excluded from the franchise: children. This is particularly troubling because children represent the future. Children comprise twenty-five percent of the population and a country can only claim to be a true democracy by allowing children to vote. Enfranchising children will also aid their socialization and allow them to represent their own interests and needs. Allowing children the right to vote and helping children realize their political goals is a moral necessity for democratic societies.

The history of suffrage has been diffusive: wealthy adult males were the first to get the vote, eventually all adult males, then women, then the young over the age of 18. Modern suffrage is a legacy from a disappearing industrial society. For more than two centuries the vote has been gradually shedding its numerous restrictions—racial, property, gender-related, etc. The last remaining restriction, age qualification, holds. Children under 18, who constitute about one quarter of the population, remain in the "black hole" of suffrage. The "black hole" in suffrage leads to a "black hole" in politics and the state. So, an outrageous unfairness towards and discrimination against children persists.

Leo Semashko, "Children's Suffrage as a Key Way of Improvement of Children's Well-being in an Age of Globalization," *Electronic Journal of Sociology*, 2004. Reproduced by permission.

Becoming a nation's citizen from birth, a child becomes a voter only after 18 years, as if in the intervening years the child lives outside society, is not its member, does not have problems and needs, and does not do anything of social importance. In fact, children do the most important thing: they reproduce themselves as a nation's major human resource, the one that is later to reproduce ALL of the nation's resources, and on which, therefore, the nation's future TOTALLY depends. *Why then don't we see deputies elected on children's behalf who will represent children's interests in the legislative organs of democratic nations? Why is it that every other population group has its interests represented, while children's interests are not represented and basically excluded from politics in general?* What accounts for this is a deeply-rooted electoral tradition, a legacy of industrial society, which allows ONLY for direct and single voting: every able-bodied citizen has only ONE vote, (s)he may vote only in person, on his/her own behalf, never on anyone else's. *Such is the major voting principle of modern democracy*, a principle formed in the industrial society. At a first superficial glance it seems quite fair. However, a closer examination reveals that this principle is fair for adults ONLY and not for children.

Politically, *children's interests must be taken into account as much as adults' interests.*

The Moral Necessity of Children's Suffrage

Children, from birth, are members of society and citizens of a nation. Like adults, they have pressing needs and engage in a wide spectrum of daily activities. They do something which is very important for society: they reproduce themselves as a major social resource. They are engaged in socializing themselves. And this activity is just as important as any other socially useful activity. Moreover, for society, the socialization of children and the younger generation is a most important life-spring, which determines society's future and its quality. The process of socialization is very difficult and arduous for every child. Children's socialization is needed not only by children but by adults, by society in general, as well. And if socialization requires an efficient political instrument, such as children's suffrage, then society should add it to its political process. So, there is a social necessity for children's suffrage.

Its political necessity arises from the fact that the political process of a democratic government is flawed and inefficient without children's suffrage, without having the vote granted to nearly a quarter of the population excluded heretofore. Democracy's completion and maturity is predicated on the completion and maturity of citizens' suffrage. Suffrage is the beginning and the fountainhead of democracy, the gateway to it, whose quality and breadth determine the quality and breadth of a democracy. Contemporary suffrage is restricted to adults, and excludes children under age 18, who make up nearly 25% of the population; and for this reason contemporary democracy, from the viewpoint of suffrage, is only 75% complete and mature. Suffrage is a principal resource for the formation of power structures in a democratic nation. And if one quarter of this source is blocked, and people—the source of power—are "shortened" by one quarter, then the quality of a democratic government is significantly lessened in comparison with the possibilities of its completion.

Helping children is a moral and psychological obligation of adults, parents and guardians above all.

Children, as well as adults, have their special interests. *Politically*, children's interests must be taken into account as much as adults' interests. Children's suffrage, secured by law, has an enormous political significance, as it broadens and deepens democracy, lending to it a child's kindly face. Through children's suffrage, democracy broadens its resource base, people, to include the totality of its population. Democracy needs children's suffrage as much as children do. Adopting children's suffrage is the only way for democracy to prove its viability and to show contemporaries that, paraphrasing Winston Churchill, although it is the worst form of government, all the others that have been tried are worse still. Such is a general political necessity of children's suffrage. Politically, suffrage must be made more inclusive.

There is also a moral and psychological need that stems from the two needs outlined above. We talked earlier about the social *unfairness* of the key principle of suffrage upheld by modern democracy, a principle that completely excludes children from politics. As is well known, because of their age, children are unable to politically articulate their interests. This principle allows adults to ignore children's interests in the electoral systems of democratic nations and to deprive children of the vote. However, children's inability to articulate their interests does not mean they should be deprived of the vote. Is it fair to deprive children of the vote only because they are unable to articulate their interests? If children's problems and interests are as important as those of adults', then, for fairness sake, *adults, rather than exclude, should incorporate children's interests into the political sphere; rather than deprive children of the vote, should give it to them.* If we are to follow this line of thinking, *adults, rather than barring children from participation in election, should HELP* them to participate, ASSUMING, as parents or legal guardians, the task of articulating children's interests by way of ELECTING fitting parliamentary deputies, who would promote children's interests in the legislative bodies of the government. Helping children is a moral and psychological obligation of adults, parents and guardians above all.

11

Youth Disenfranchisement Equals Taxation Without Representation

Pro-Youth Pages

Pro-Youth Pages offers a series of articles on youth related subjects including the arts, the news media, and public policy.

Traditional political philosophy has stated that the citizens of democratic states should only be held accountable to laws that they have had a voice in forming. In the United States, however, adolescents under 18 are held accountable to laws, even though they are unable to vote. One glaring example of exclusion is taxes. All youth, regardless of age, pay taxes, despite having no representation. In fact, taxation without representation was the central issue leading to the American Revolution. Traditionally, those deemed too young to understand breaking a law (like shoplifting) would not be held accountable for breaking that law. In the United States, however, adolescents as young as 14 are eligible for the death penalty. One solution to this unfairness is to lower the voting age, allowing young Americans to play a role in shaping the nation's laws.

[T]homas] Hobbes, [John] Locke, and other great political philosophers agreed that when human beings first left the state of nature to create civilization, they were entering into a "social contract." In any contract, each party agrees to give up certain things in return for certain benefits. When hu-

Pro-Youth Pages, "Disenfranchised," May 14, 2007. www.geocities.com/hatredsucks. Reproduced by permission.

mans first entered into a social contract, they gained, for example, protection of their property against thieves, in return for which they gave up the freedom to take whatever they pleased.

With every right people gain through the social contract, people also take on certain obligations. When a group of people are singled out to be denied a right, however, it would seem only fair that group remain free of the obligations tied to the right they've been denied. Yet in America today, youth are denied many rights and are still expected to shoulder the responsibilities associated with those rights.

Youth, for example, are denied the right to file law-suits. In some states, a youth who has the energy and know-how can jump through legal hoops and get a lawyer to file on his behalf, but youths do not enjoy the same free access to the courts enjoyed by their elders. Adults, however, can still sue children and teenagers as easily as they can sue other adults. Is this fair? Should someone with no right to file his own lawsuits be saddled with the obligation to answer lawsuits?

This essay, however, will focus on the right to vote and the obligations tied to that right. I offer these comments as food for thought as we search for a fairer way to treat youth.

Taxation Without Representation

In the United States, there is no age-limit on the obligation to pay taxes. Anyone with a job sees tax money deducted from his paycheck: for federal income taxes, for social security taxes, and for other taxes. Even the child with no job is required to pay sales taxes, road tolls, and other payments to the government. Yet, while no state has an age-limit on being taxed, every state has an age-limit on voting.

Are voting and taxes tied together? Absolutely. When someone buys stock in a corporation, he is entitled to a vote in how that corporation is run. Likewise, when someone pays money into his government, he is entitled to a voice in how that money is spent. This connection should be clear to every American. Our nation was founded on the motto "No taxation without representation." By "representation," our founders meant election of law-makers who represent our views.

For 200 years before the Revolution, Americans lived as colonists under British rule. Unlike citizens of Britain, these colonists had no vote in deciding who could sit in Parliament. The colonists accepted this, however, because they also had no obligation to pay taxes to Britain. The French and Indian War changed that.

When Native Americans, backed by the powerful French army, challenged colonists for the land, the colonists urged Britain's King George III to send his mighty army to fight for the colonies. King George III did so, and the British army triumphed.

The King found waging war expensive. Hoping to recoup his loses, the King taxed those people he believed had benefited the most from this military expenditure: the colonists. This caused outrage. Yes, the colonists had benefited from the King's expenditure, but they had no say in how that money was spent and therefore, they reasoned, the money should not be taken from their pockets. For this, they went to war, demanding independence.

In the Declaration of Independence, our founders declared that governments derive their just power from the "consent of the governed."

In the same year that Thomas Jefferson wrote our *Declaration of Independence*, he also drafted a constitution for the state of virginia. In his draft, any Virginia-resident who had paid taxes to the state for at least two years would be guaranteed the right to vote, regardless of race, gender, or age. Jefferson was no egalitarian; his draft also guaranteed voting rights to "male persons of full age" regardless of whether they had paid taxes. But while Jefferson did not believe in full equality, he understood it was wrong to demand taxes from people who had no vote in how that money would be used. Likewise today it would seem only fair that those who are locked out of the voting booth should also be free of the obligation to pay taxes.

Voting and Laws

As John Adams prepared his contributions to the American Revolution, he received a letter from his wife, the intellectual Abigail Adams. She urged him that, in shaping this new nation, he should give voting rights to women because women "will not hold ourselves bound by any laws in which we have no voice or representation."

There has never been a time when Americans did not acknowledge this basic truth, that a law can only be imposed fairly on those who had some say in shaping that law. In the *Declaration of Independence*, our founders declared that governments derive their just power from the "consent of the governed." Even earlier, Puritan leader John Winthrop, speaking in 1639 as the deputy governor of the Massachusetts colony, described the relationship between government and the governed by comparing it to the relationship between a husband and wife: "The woman's own choice makes such a man her husband; yet being so chosen, he is her lord, and she is subject to him." While Winthrop was revealing a horribly patriarchal view of the family, he was acknowledging that only those who have chosen an authority have any obligation to obey that authority. This sentiment surfaced again when feminist Susan B. Anthony denounced "man-made, unjust, unconstitutional forms of law that tax, fine, imprison, and hang women while they deny them the right of representation in the government;" and the sentiment surfaced again when Martin Luther King wrote in his Letter from Birmingham Jail, "A law is unjust if it is inflicted on a minority that, as a result of being denied the right to vote, had no part in enacting or devising the law."

Children Are Not Exempt From the Law

Should those declared too young to vote be exempt from obeying laws? This sounds like a shocking idea, yet to an extent, it is already followed. If a four-year-old in a supermarket puts something in his pocket and wanders away, we do not prosecute the child as a shoplifter. We assume a four-year-old lacks the sophistication to fully understand the ramifications of shoplifting, to understand the violation of property rights and its impact on victims. For that reason, we do not jail the four-year-old and, for the same reason, we do not give the four-year-old a voice in shaping public policy regarding shoplifting. Since he cannot understand the ramifications of shoplifting, he cannot reasonably judge how our society should treat shoplifters any more than he can reasonably judge whether he himself should shoplift. But as the youth becomes older, we expect him to reach a degree of sophistication where he does understand the ramifications of shoplifting. At that point, if he still chooses to steal, we punish him for that choice. But if someone has that degree of sophistication, it follows that he is sophisticated enough to help shape the laws on shoplifting, help to determine its proper punishment. If he cannot understand shoplifting well enough to have a say in how we should treat shoplifters, then he cannot understand it well enough to be held accountable if he himself becomes a shoplifter. The same holds true for any other crime.

Yet all across America, we build juvenile halls for the sole purpose of punishing those not allowed to vote. Americans as young as 14 are eligible for the death penalty, held to the highest level of responsibility, while declared not responsible enough to cast a vote.

We allow a young law-breaker to be tried "as an adult" if a prosecutor decides this particular youth is responsible enough to be treated as such. Why is there no similar procedure for law-abiding youth who want to vote? Can it be that the only youth who are responsible and sophisticated are the ones who commit crimes? I find that unlikely.

Lowering the Voting Age

I see two ways our society can act honorably on this question. One is to treat people on an individual basis: decide which individuals are responsible enough to vote and to be held responsible for crimes, and leave the remaining individuals devoid of votes or responsibility. The other way is to break people into age-groups. Those age-groups considered responsible will be allowed to vote and will be held responsible for any crimes they commit. The remaining age-groups will have no voice and bear no legal responsibility.

If the second path is taken, this would result in raising the age at which one can be punished for crimes, or lowering the age at which one can vote, or both.

Democracy is built on a belief in fairness.

The idea of lowering the voting age probably scares many adults, though I'm not sure why it should. In the early 1970's, the voting age in America was lowered by three years, from 21 to 18. The impact this had on our society was minimal. It led to a temporary drop in the legal drinking age to 18, but in the next decade, the drinking age was restored to 21.

If the voting age were lowered again, to 14 for example, there is little likelihood this would have much impact on those older than 18. The older group would still hold the majority of votes; nothing could be done without their support. So why should Americans fear lowering the voting age to match the age of accountability, the age at which we expect people to bear full responsibility for their actions?

The Cornerstone of Democracy

Some insist teenagers should not be trusted with even a small portion of the votes because teenagers are intellectually inferior to adults. For those people, I refer you once more to that great American founding father Thomas Jefferson.

Jefferson felt the same way about blacks. In his book *Notes on the State of Virginia*, Jefferson wrote several pages describing his view of blacks, insisting they were inferior to whites in knowledge, intellect, reason, imagination, and in other respects. Yet later, this same man wrote of blacks, "whatever be their degree of talent, it is no measure of their rights. Because Sir Isaac Newton was superior to others in understanding, he was not therefore lord of the person or property of others". Even the "inferior" classes of people should have a say in the laws they obey, or else be relieved of the obligation to obey them: this is the cornerstone doctrine of democracy.

Aristocracy is built on the belief that the most educated people should shape laws for all to obey. Democracy is built on a belief in fairness.

12

Youth Must Study Citizenship Before Voting

Hans Zeiger

Hans Zeiger is the author of Reagan's Children: Taking Back the City on the Hill *and* Get Off My Honor: The Assault on the Boy Scouts of America.

Recently, a number of organizations like the Association for Children's Suffrage have advocated lowering the voting age. American society, however, has long associated adulthood with the age of 18; because of this, the idea of lowering the voting age remains far outside the mainstream. Many who support lowering the voting age have forgotten the value of a solid civics education. Education, not lowering the voting age, will provide young Americans with the necessary foundation for citizenship.

On the day of the California presidential primary last month, six Berkeley high-school students woke up early to protest the constitutional voting age outside of a local polling place. Instead of suffrage at 18, the high-school students propose a voting age of 16.

"Got ballots?" asked one homemade picket sign, while another read, "No taxation without representation. Where's my ballot?!?" Before going to school, the students marched inside the polling place to demand a ballot, but a volunteer turned them away.

I contacted the 17-year-old protest leader, Robert Reynolds, the local chapter leader of a small radical youth movement called National Youth Rights Association, and I asked the problem with the status quo. "Politicians have no reason to pay attention to the interests of teenagers because teenagers are nothing to them because they can't vote," Reynolds said.

The National Youth Rights Association proposes a voting age of 16 while a more extreme group, called Americans for a Free Society from Age Restrictions, says, "A Constitutional amendment forbidding the right to vote to be denied on the basis of age should be proposed and sent to the states for ratification." A similar mission led to the founding of a Brown University student organization called the Association for Children's Suffrage.

Fortunately, the concept of children voting remains far from the mainstream. In the cases of proposed unregulated enfranchisement, a child's right to vote is comparable to allowing cats and dogs to vote.

Nevertheless, Reynolds is convinced that the Constitution will be amended to allow children to vote during his lifetime. "I will still be working on it until the voting age is lowered," he promises.

Under the original U.S. Constitution, the voting age was set at 21. It was at 21 that a young person became an official adult in the Western tradition. English common law established the age of 21 as the minimum eligibility for knighthood.

The reason all of America has compulsory education is so that it can train students in the great study of citizenship.

Throughout time, all societies have recognized the important distinction between childhood and adulthood. (The concept of "adolescence" is only a century old.) While it is true that in some societies adulthood comes sooner than in others, American childhood does not fully merge into adulthood until the completion of formal education and eligibility for military service at age 18. Hence the 26th Amendment to the Constitution in 1972 that lowered the voting age from 21 to 18.

Since 1972, relatively little has changed in the timing of major life transitions for young Americans. Age 18 is the typical age of movement between high school and college, civilian and military, living with parents and living independently.

Education and Citizenship

The concept of children voting is not a symptom or political necessity in conformity to America's republican form of government. It is rather a symptom of generational confusion, a bewilderment more pronounced in the moral culture than it is in discussions of politics.

In our time, the social roles of adults and children have been increasingly questioned. Young people who are immersed in the relativist values of the culture are blinded to the necessity of boundaries between childhood and adulthood. Instead of young people aspiring in due time to the values, norms and types of entertainment of their parents, they are trying to rush the maturity process.

Reynolds says that education has nothing to do with the right to vote. "In the Constitution, it doesn't say anything about having to have an education before you can vote," he says.

But America's founders were convinced that education has much to do with civic responsibility. "Religion, morality, and knowledge" are prerequisites to "good government and the happiness of mankind," wrote the authors of the 1787 Northwest Ordinance, and thus, "schools and the means of education shall be forever encouraged."

The reason all of America has compulsory education is so that it can train students in the great study of citizenship.

We've forgotten that. But indeed, education does come before the vote. Concerned America ought to be more worried about the content of our educational system than about flimsy, temporary get out the vote drives. We should spend more energy teaching American history and civics than we do struggling to resist those who come to power devoid of genuine history and civics education. Citizenship is a product of education.

Children aren't about to vote, but America's prevailing spirit of radical egalitarianism is becoming more and more extreme day by day. If current trends keep up, our generation will be fighting the battle over under-aged voting within a few decades.

13

Mock Voting For Kids Encourages Adult Voting

Meg Chorlian

Meg Chorlian writes for Cobblestone *and is the author of* The Korean War: 1950–1953.

Although children under 18 are not allowed to vote in the United States, a program called Kids Voting USA (KVUSA) has allowed children a chance to simulate the voting experience. The KVUSA program operates in a number of states, allowing children from kindergarten to high school to cast mock votes at official polling places. Studies have shown that when participants in KVUSA have reached 18, they vote at higher rates than students who did not participate in the program. Furthermore, KVUSA participants have higher voter participation throughout their voting lives.

So, you just don't understand why voting is so important? Don't mention that to Paula Case or anyone else associated with Kids Voting USA (KVUSA). KVUSA is an organization that offers an authentic voting experience for anyone under the age of eighteen. With programs in more than thirty states, Kids Voting USA is demonstrating the value of the vote to students from kindergarten through twelfth grade.

Case, director of communications at KVUSA, says, "One of the very best things about KVUSA is that the classroom activities make learning about citizenship fun. And, I really enjoy meeting Kids Voting students who have acquired the skills and confidence to address something they felt was important in their community or our country." Case shared some other thoughts about Kids Voting USA with COBBLESTONE.

Cobblestone: How and when did kids voting USA get started?

Paula Case: The idea for Kids Voting USA began in 1987, when three Arizona businessmen went to Costa Rica on a fishing trip. They learned that this Central American country enjoyed a voter turnout rate of about eighty percent. A tradition of youth visiting the polls with parents on Election Day primarily was credited for the high turnout. When the three men returned to Arizona, they decided to create a program in the Phoenix area that would encourage American kids to go to the polls with their parents on Election Day.

Kids Take Part in the Political Process

How does the organization work?

A Kids Voting program involves every aspect of a community. It is led by a board of volunteer community leaders. Organizations and businesses provide funding, election officials make an Election Day experience possible, and teachers offer activities. Students prepare for Election Day in the classroom. They learn information-gathering and decision-making skills, how the political process impacts daily life, and how they play an important role in that process. The program also encourages parent-child interaction and discussion. Students are asked to talk with the adults in their lives about early voting experiences and the general political process.

Do kids really get to vote?

On Election Day, students are invited to official polling places to cast a Kids Voting ballot alongside the adults. Kindergarten through sixth-grade students must be accompanied by an adult. The kids' ballot has the same races and issues as the adult ballot, but with pictures [of the candidates] so the youngest kids also can participate. The ballot is divided into sections that enable kindergarten through second-grade students to vote on certain races, third- through fifth-grade students to vote on a majority of races, and middle and high school students to vote on the entire ballot, including issues.

Recent research indicates that when students receive a compelling civics education, it leads to greater participation throughout their adult lives.

As the adult voting process changes, so does Kids Voting. More and more students now take part in early voting and mail-in balloting. There also have been computer and on-line voting pilot projects.

How are votes tallied? Are they published?

Each Kids Voting community has its own tabulation process. Many use standardized ballot forms, which can be scanned and computer tabulated. Some smaller programs enjoy the process of hand-counting votes and make it a community event.

All results are reported to the media just as official results are. Kids Voting programs also provide results to each school that participates.

Mock Voting Increases Voter Turnout

How has Kids Voting USA seen that its program is working?

Research conducted in Kansas showed that eighteen-year-old Kids Voting participants registered to vote at a rate that was five percent higher than that of their non-participating peers. And even more impressive, they voted at a rate fourteen percent higher than non-Kids Voting participants. Independent research also has shown that communities with Kids Voting programs see a three to five percent increase in adult voter turnout.

Why do you think it is important to get kids at this age involved in voting?

We're learning that young adults don't participate because they think one person can't make a difference, that the polling place is a mystery to them, and that they don't have the knowledge and skills needed to be fully involved citizens. Recent research indicates that when students receive a compelling civics education, it leads to greater participation throughout their adult lives. By providing relevant and fun citizenship activities, Kids Voting USA is offering young people the knowledge and skills necessary for living in a participatory democracy.

14

Civics Education Should Precede the Right to Vote

Dean Esmay

Dean Esmay operates Dean's World, *a Web site defending the liberal tradition in history, science, and philosophy.*

In the past, the franchise was often withheld from new groups for a good reason: citizens feared that new voters would not take the responsibility of voting seriously. During the national debate over women's suffrage, there were men who supported the idea of women voting and women who opposed it. The anti-suffragettes, for instance, believed that women were incapable of assuming the heavy responsibility of voting. Still, once women had won the vote, the anti-suffragettes joined forces with the suffragettes to form the League of Women Voters: responsible voting was more important than political differences. Young Americans who wish to vote before 18 should first learn about their government and about contemporary issues. Only when these adolescents have been able to prove their political competence within the school classroom should they be allowed to vote.

Kim Swygert finds the idea of 14 year old voters ridiculous. Allow me to dissent, at least for the sake of a thought experiment:

Throughout the 19th century, as the franchise was extended to more and more people, those who opposed extending the vote to non-property owners, to non-whites, to women, etc. generally argued that these groups should not be

Dean Esmay, "Dean's World: Responsible Exercise of the Franchise," *Dean's World*, May 11, 2004. www.deanesmay.com/archives/000190.html. Reproduced by permission.

given the vote because they would not be responsible with it. Sure, underlying it was some bigoted assumptions, but ultimately the argument was always the same: were these people responsible enough to take the vote seriously?

While it may seem self-evident that these were bigoted viewpoints, it's easy to just stop there. "Wow, bigots didn't want the 'wrong people' voting." But if that's all you see you're missing an important point: quite often those who opposed extending the franchise were worried that *people would be irresponsible with their votes.*

In our early 21st century mindset, we tend to focus on how "oppressive" it was that all those groups were once denied the "right" to vote. But in the context of the 19th century especially it wasn't clear to everybody that the vote was a "right." Generally, voting was seen as a duty, and a heavy responsibility. So, whenever it was proposed that the franchise be extended to a new group, the debate generally centered primarily on whether this new group would be *responsible* or *thoughtful*, as opposed to *selfish* or *stupid*, with its votes.

An episode from history helps to illustrate this point: A modern mythology surrounding the 19th and early 20th century holds that people like Susan B. Anthony and Elizabeth Cady Stanton and the entire Suffragette movement were progressive visionaries bravely fighting oppressive male society, wresting the vote from men who selfishly wished to keep women oppressed.

But here's the truth: while we don't have statistical samples to give us meaningful polling data, we can look at the literature from the debates during that era and note that, quite often, men thought that giving women the vote was a perfectly reasonable idea—and, quite often, women thought the idea utterly daft.

You may be wondering where I'm going with all this. Just stick with me.

The Anti-Suffragettes

A forgotten—very wrongly forgotten, and wrongly dismissed—group of women who ought to be considered feminist icons were known as *The Anti-Suffragists* (or "Anti-Suffragettes" or just plain "Antis."). Many of them wrote pamphlets, articles, and entire books opposing the concept of female suffrage. Not because they believed in inherent feminine inferiority, but for a complex set of reasons which tended to boil down to the notion that women were superior within the home environment and inferior in the outer world of politics, and that the reverse was true for men.

Their reasoning seems backward today. But these were often women with college degrees, and some of them were engaged in full-time outside-the-home professions. Most of them were powerful, self-assured women with many admirable qualities that made them true community leaders. Ida Tarbell and Helen Kendrick Johnson are particularly fascinating to me, but there were quite a few others. These were often women who wrote and spoke passionately on the subject, with their message basically saying, "those Women's Suffragists are nuts!"

Here's the bottom line: We have forgotten the concept of responsible exercise of the franchise.

They sometimes even disagreed with their husbands on the issue. Tarbell seems even to have been a lesbian, which I find even more fascinating.

Now, let me be clear that I do not believe the Anti-Suffragettes were right. But their reasoning was that the vote was a very heavy-duty responsibility, and that the typical female mind was unsuited to it. Yes, that seems very backward and primitive. But shove past that: what all these people were arguing over was whether the vote would be *used responsibly* by women. The Anti-Suffragettes did not argue that women were inferior, just that they wouldn't *vote responsibly*. The Suffragettes, on the other hand, spent enormous amounts of time arguing that women *would* use the vote responsibly, maybe even *more* responsibly than men....

While basic *fairness* was part of the core message of the Suffragettes, it was just as important to most of them to prove that women could and would *vote responsibly* and *contribute meaningfully.*

Are you catching my drift yet? If not I'll try to spell it out again: for the people involved in this and similar debates over giving more and more people the vote, this was as much a struggle argument over *how to make sure the franchise was exercised in a responsible way* as anything else.

Again, underlying it all: voting is *a grave responsibility.*

The Responsibility of Voting

Here's a fascinating tidbit that underscores all that for me: after the Suffragettes won the day and the 19th Amendment passed, many of them teamed up with their former Anti-Suffragette opponents to form an organization called the League of Women Voters.

That's right, many of the women who opposed women's suffrage got involved in the League of Women Voters.

Why? Because both sides in that debate viewed voting as a huge responsibility. So after they were done shooting it out, they shook hands like gentlemen (heh) and teamed up to make sure that all these new women voters would become well-informed, and thoughtful, and make positive contributions.

Somewhere along the line we have forgotten all this. We've come to think of voting as a "civil right," and end it there. Indeed, there's a sort of semi-mystical mindset that's taken hold that says that, somehow, the nation would be better off if more people just walked into a voting booth and randomly picked out a name. As if just showing up and pulling a lever makes the country a better place.

That's exactly what those who opposed giving blacks and women the vote said would happen, by the way. That blacks, women, non-property-owners, etc. would not take the vote seriously enough to educate themselves and put a lot of thought into their choices, and would be easily swayed by lies and emotional rhetoric. Isn't that kind of sad?

Before you get into a voting booth, you should understand government. You should understand the issues of the day.

Here's the bottom line: *We have forgotten the concept of responsible exercise of the franchise.* No one teaches their kids that it is an awesome responsibility anymore.

This, to me, is a damned shame.

Education Is Essential to Voting

So let's fast forward to today. Might there be some value in extending the franchise to High Schoolers? Well here's my little thought-experiment:

Let's say that we enacted a pilot program in one state—could be California could be any other state—which said that if you take, oh, let's say 9 credit hours of classes on Constitutional law, American social history, and civics, and pass with a "B" or better, you can be issued a voter's registration card, and you can vote even if you're under 18.

Note that I do include civics classes in the mix. Civics being the study of the nuts-and-bolts of government, as well as an overview of the major and minor political parties and their governing philosophies and positions.

This could, properly structured, start to instill in young people an attitude, a mentality that says, "Before you get into a voting booth you should understand government. You should understand the issues of the day. You should know something about the major parties and some of the minor parties. You should know the candidates. You should grasp what an awesome responsibility government is, and how incredible self-government is."

Those kids who did put the work in to do that might well serve to shame some of their fellows—not to mention some adults—into treating government, and their vote, a little more seriously.

Odd as it sounds, properly structured, a program to give teenagers the vote like this might well be a step in the right direction.

15

Adolescents Are Too Lazy to Vote

Tom Kemp

Tom Kemp writes for the Daily Telegraph.

While some people have suggested lowering the voting age to 16, these people clearly do not understand the British teenager. In fact, looking at a teenager's bedroom will make his flaws clear. From the covered, messy floor strewn with towels and clothes, it is easy to comprehend that the British teen is quite lazy. A further survey of his room reveals a number of electronic items including an Xbox, stereo, and television, informing us that the British teen is also very expensive to maintain. The British teen prefers sleeping late on the weekends and has little interest in political issues. Still, there is nothing wrong with giving the teenager the vote, as long as his or her father is allowed to cast that vote until he or she is 21.

I notice that David Miliband, the minister who suggested this week [February 2004] that the voting age should be brought down to 16, is himself only 38 and has no teenagers of his own. He would be wise to get to know the species before he presses ahead with his lunatic scheme. I am therefore happy to offer him an inspection of my own 16-year-old son, who is as typical a specimen as he will find.

The Great British Teenager (GBT) is best studied in his natural habitat. In my son's case, this is a room at the back of the house, with walls painted a very dark and shiny blue. (His first choice of colour scheme—black walls and orange ceiling—was vetoed by his parents.)

Before Mr Miliband ventures inside, he should take a deep breath and hold a handkerchief to his nose and mouth. This is because the GBT likes to live in a fug of rich aromas, given off by cheesy socks, muddy rugby kit and the fungus-encrusted remains of forgotten pizzas.

The first thing that the minister will notice, once his eyes have become accustomed to the gloom, is that every inch of the floor is piled high with discarded clothes, wet towels, exercise books, dirty mugs, guitar music, CDs, cereal bowls, video games and magazines.

I read a survey last autumn, which said that British teenagers much preferred apples to oranges, simply because they didn't have to go to the trouble of peeling them.

Mr Miliband will already be half-way towards learning his first important lesson about the GBT: he is a phenomenally lazy creature, incapable of doing anything for himself. The wet towels are there, abandoned where they fell, because returning them to the towel rail would mean a three-yard walk to the bathroom. The laundry basket is a full yard farther away, on the landing. For the GBT, it might as well be in New South Wales.

He would never contemplate the journey to the bathroom or the laundry basket while there remained the slightest possibility that his mother would tidy everything away, and save him the bother. Still less would he make the great trek all the way downstairs to the kitchen, to return all that cutlery and crockery.

I read a survey last autumn, which said that British teenagers much preferred apples to oranges, simply because they didn't have to go trouble of peeling them. The childless may have thought that was a joke, or at least a wild exaggeration. But parents of teenagers all over the country will testify that it is the unvarnished truth.

The Lazy British Teen

The next thing Mr Miliband will notice about the GBT's lair is the astonishing amount of electrical equipment that it contains. There are cables everywhere, spewing from the Xbox and the television, the guitar amplifier, the video recorder, the stereo system and the radio-alarm clock.

The minister will be on his way to learning the second great truth about the GBT: that he is fabulously expensive to maintain. Everything in his lair has been paid for by the poor bloody worker—most of it by his father, but the rest by over-indulgent grandmothers, aunts and godparents. The GBT knows that it is extremely important that he should have the very latest bloodthirsty video game. But it would never occur to him that he should be required to pay for it by his own efforts.

Mr Miliband will have learnt these two truths about the GBT even before he has met the beast. Indeed, standing there in my 16-year-old's room, he will probably think he is entirely alone. But if he visits us at the weekend, before about 2pm, I can assure him that the GBT will be there. It is just that he won't feel it is quite the time to get up yet.

My solution is that all children should be given a vote—but until they are 21, their votes should be cast by their fathers.

The minister should study the misshapen lump under the duvet, and give it a sharp prod. I find that the best implement for this is a broom handle, since the GBT can turn nasty if anybody who tries to rouse him is within striking distance. The first prod usually elicits a grunt. The second a groan, and a muffled oath.

At this point, Mr Miliband may assume that the GBT is awake. He may then try to ask him about his views on foundation hospitals, Network Rail, the euro, the Anglo-American alliance and the future of the BBC. If he is lucky, he will be answered by a series of grunts and a semi-articulate inquiry about his sanity. If he is unlucky, the GBT will storm out of the room, cursing and slamming the door.

It is utterly absurd that Mr Miliband should contemplate giving my 16-year-old the vote. The idea that the lump under the duvet should be given any say in how much tax I should pay, on top of his upkeep, fills me with the deepest horror.

But I agree that children are part of society, and that they ought to be represented in some way. My solution is that all children should be given a vote—but until they are 21, their votes should be cast by their fathers.

16

Politically Engaged Adolescents Should Be Allowed to Vote

Libby Brooks

Libby Brooks is the author of The Story of Childhood: Growing Up in Modern Britain.

British youth, despite a popularly held belief by adults, are interested in politics. In 2003, many British youths participated in anti-war demonstrations, even though they were too young to vote. There is little support for lowering the voting age, however, either by adults or by adolescents themselves. Adults frequently accuse teens of disinterest while teens openly wonder if they have enough knowledge to vote. The problem, though, rests with a generational shift, not a lack of knowledge. Adolescents are less interested in ideology and less likely to approach politics in a traditional manner. As a result, British youth may choose to attend a demonstration, but may respond cynically to a traditional activity referred to as "political." Far from diluting the voting process, lowering the voting age will allow British adults a chance to listen to new solutions from the next generation.

In the spring of 2003, on the first day of the invasion of Iraq, Britain was witness to a new kind of protest. In the most significant youth-led campaign for a century, schoolchildren as young as 10 walked out of their classrooms to attend what were, for most, their first political demonstrations.

Libby Brooks, "We Can Have Sex, So Why Can't We Vote?" *Guardian*, February 28, 2006, p. 12. Copyright © 2006 Guardian News & Media Ltd. Reproduced by permission of Guardian News Service Ltd.

I spent the day in London's Parliament Square. By lunchtime, the atmosphere was rowdy but festive. Cigarettes were smoked, slyly, cupped in hands held behind backs. Boys checked out girls, checking out boys, chanting, "Who let the bombs off? Bush! Bush and Blair!"

By late afternoon, several thousand young people had gathered, the majority of them under 16. These young people had organised themselves, leafleting at school gates, recruiting via email networks and cultivating the attentions of the media. Their understanding of how the news worked and their alertness to propaganda was impressive. These children were sceptical, but not cynical, and well informed about why they were there.

At the time, adults struggled to identify the causes of this extraordinary surge of activism. Surely the younger generation was apathetic? Didn't kids care about celebrities, consumer goods and animals, and only then if they were cute enough? The adolescent idealism which had blossomed amid the radical politics of the 60s and 70s was now limited to the occasional prisoner of conscience. These assemblies were dismissed as a short-lived trendification of protest, fuelled by mass hysteria and the lure of legitimised misbehaviour.

Treat them like citizens and they will act as such.

Two years later, in the early summer of 2005, many of the children I spoke to in Parliament Square would by then have been old enough to have sex, get married and join the armed forces with their parents' consent, work and—crucially—pay taxes. But they were not old enough to vote in the general election of May 5 that year. While the rest of the million or so marchers against the war had the opportunity to make explicit their feelings of anger and impotence at the ballot box, young people had no chance to make this most basic of connections.

Should the Voting Age Be Lowered?

Lowering the voting age to 16 has been mooted a number of times as a way of countering public disengagement from politics. When the chancellor, Gordon Brown, signalled his support for the idea February 27, 2006, he will have affronted many who argue that reducing the voting age will simply increase the number of people who don't vote. British teenagers are far too busy happy-slapping, smoking psychosis-inducing skunk or gaining easy exam passes to be bothered reading a manifesto.

Indeed, many adults believe that children today have too many rights already, perhaps because they confuse rights with consumerism and pester power. They fear that "rights" mean children "divorcing" their parents if they don't get what they want, or mindlessly grabbing more than their fair share of adult power. It is assumed that children won't make rational choices if they are allowed to make decisions for themselves.

This is a generation growing up in a political climate that has, for better or worse, moved beyond ideologies.

This kind of damned-if-you-do, damned-if-don't argument runs like a seam through discussions about contemporary childhood. Young people are granted rights in principle by the [United Nations] Charter on the Rights of the Child, but refused many of them in practice. They are denied responsibility over their own education, health and welfare hand then they are punished when they behave irresponsibly. They are excluded from the political process, then berated for their apathy.

Certainly, there seems to be minimal public support for lowering the voting age—polling at the time of the Electoral Commission found that only 25% of adults wanted the age lowered. Nor do young people's voting habits initially suggest it's a worthwhile move: in the 2005 election, national turnout was 61%, compared with 37% among 18- to 24-year-olds, down 2% from 2001.

But a more detailed examination seems to indicate that if you give young people the vote early, then their democratic engagement will increase. Treat them like citizens and they will act as such. Research by YouGov and the Social Market Foundation into how people develop voting habits has found that those who are old enough to vote while still at school are more likely to vote again than those who have to wait until their 20s for their first chance. In the 2001 election, for example, turnout among 27-year-olds was 49%, compared with 65% among 28-year-olds who had been old enough to vote in the 1992 election.

One of the reasons the Electoral Commission gave for rejecting the proposal was that young people themselves were divided on the issue. But lack of confidence in their knowledge of the political system is not the same as apathy. For example, research by Nottingham Trent University found that 71% of people who were aged 18 at the time of the 2001 election felt that there weren't enough opportunities for young people to influence government. But 60% also said that they were nervous about voting because they didn't feel they knew enough.

A New Political Climate

This is a generation growing up in a political climate that has, for better or worse, moved beyond ideologies. Belief systems are no longer thrashed out at the kitchen table. The only voting intention passed on from parent to child these days is the intention not to vote at all, because it's not just adolescents who think that politics is boring or irrelevant to their lives. The places where people used to come together to make a difference, the church hall or the union meeting, are now empty of adults as well as young people. But the success of those flashes of mass education provided by Live 8 or the anti-war movement indicate that the appetite is still there.

Clearly, this is where citizenship classes could be providing a more structured focus for that political education. Indeed, the Electoral Commission believed that the most powerful argument in favour of lowering the voting age was that school leavers could address their new right to vote in their citizenship classes, which became compulsory in the autumn of 2002. The largest ever survey of pupils' opinions on their citizenship classes, published last year, found that, while most enjoyed the subject, 67% of students said that they remained uninterested in politics.

This was inevitably reported as further confirmation of young people's apathy. But what the survey actually showed was that while young people continued to mistrust politicians and had minimal interest in participating in traditional politics, less conventional forms of participation were far more popular. Fifty-three per cent of those polled had taken part in a range of political activities, including signing petitions, attending public meetings and taking part in demonstrations. Seventy-five per cent of year-12 pupils indicated that they intended to vote in the future, and 68% read a national newspaper, while many more watched the news on television, and a fifth used the internet to look up current affairs.

Perhaps the disparity between interest in world events and interest in the political structure comes down to language. The very mention of "politics" puts many young people off. It is worth noting that Newsround, consistently the most watched terrestrial children's programme, seldom uses the P-word or reports on the day-to-day running of parliament, concentrating instead on single issues.

Listen to Youth

Young people's focus on single issues is often cited with mild derision, suggesting that they are political consumerists and naifs, swayed by the most self-serving or popular issues, too lazy to get to grips with the intricacies of international relations or trade agreements that underpin war or famine. But is a 16-year-old with plenty to say about antisocial behaviour or bullying so different from the 46-year-old who is concerned about her tax banding?

It has been suggested that lowering the voting age would inevitably benefit the Labour party, but recent research by a number of organisations has found the younger generation to be rather more conservative on issues such as immigration and crime than their elders. The teen vote remains very much up for grabs.

For a country that often appears to pride itself on how much it worries about its younger generation, we are remarkably bad at listening to what it has to say. Perhaps adults find it harder to recognise young people's political involvement because it is happening in the entirely new context of an accelerated consumer society. Nick Barham, who interviewed hundreds of teenagers for his book *Disconnected*, notes that they were most engaged when responding to the branded homogeneity of "youth culture": this ranged from making outfits for club nights rather than shopping for the latest labels, to hosting websites to making music and short films rather than relying on going to see a Hollywood blockbuster.

The UN Charter for the Rights of the Child makes provision for the recognition of young people's "evolving capacity". Of course, some 16-year-olds are more politically agile than others, but giving them the vote need not result in a slippery slope down to industrial tribunals for toddlers. When young people are asked what they think, when they are heard, they don't just ask for less homework.

Organizations to Contact

The editors have compiled the following list of organizations concerned with the issues debated in this book. The descriptions are derived from materials provided by the organizations. All have publications or information available for interested readers. The list was compiled on the date of publication of the present volume; the information provided here may change. Be aware that many organizations take several weeks or longer to respond to inquiries, so allow as much time as possible.

American Civil Liberties Union (ACLU)
125 Broad St., 18th Floor, New York, NY   10004
(212) 549-2500 • fax: (212) 549-2646
e-mail: aclu@aclu.org
Web site: www.aclu.org

The ACLU is a national organization that defends Americans' civil rights as guaranteed in the U.S. Constitution. It advocates for freedom of all forms of speech, including pornography, flag-burning, and political protest. The ACLU offers numerous reports, fact sheets, and policy statements on free speech issues, which are freely available on its Web site. Some of these publications include "Free Speech Under Fire," "Freedom of Expression," and, for students, "Ask Sybil Liberty About Your Right to Free Expression."

American Enterprise Institute (AEI)
1150 Seventeenth St. NW, Washington, DC   20036
(202) 862-5800 • fax: (202) 862-7177
Web site: www.aei.org

The American Enterprise Institute (AEI) is a public policy institute that sponsors research and provides commentary on a wide variety of issues, including economics, social welfare, and government tax and regulatory policies. The AEI publishes the bimonthly magazine *American Enterprise* and the *AEI Newsletter.*

Brennan Center for Justice at NYU School of Law
161 Avenue of the Americas, 12th Floor
New York, NY   10013
(212) 998-6733 • fax: (212) 995-4550
Web site: www.fepproject.org

The Brennan Center for Justice is a non-partisan public policy and law institute that focuses on the fundamental issues of democracy and justice. The Brennan Center for Justice's work ranges from voting rights to redistricting reform, from access to the courts to presidential power in the fight against terrorism. The Brennan Center combines scholarship, legislative and legal advocacy, and communications to win meaningful, measurable change in the public sector.

British Youth Council (BYC)
The Mezzanine 2, Downstream Building   SE1 9BG
Web site: www.byc.org.uk

The British Youth Council (BYC) promotes the active citizenship of young people and works to develop young people's skills to participate in decision-making and controlling resources. The BYC has over 180 youth organisations in its membership and a network of over 400 Local Youth Councils.

The Brookings Institution
1775 Massachusetts Ave. NW, Washington, DC   20036-2188
(202) 797-6000 • fax: (202) 797-6004

Founded in 1927, the Brookings Institution is a liberal think tank conducts research and provides education in government, foreign policy, economics, and the social sciences. The institute publishes the *Brookings Review* quarterly, as well as numerous books and research papers.

Center for a New American Dream
6930 Carroll Avenue, Suite 900, Takoma Park, MD   20912
(301) 891-3683

e-mail: newdream@newdream.org
Web site: www.newdream.org

The Center for a New American Dream is an organization whose goal is to help Americans consume responsibly and thus protect the earth's resources and improve the quality of life. Its Kids and Commercialism Campaign provides information on the effects of advertising on children. The center publishes booklets and a quarterly newsletter, *Enough*.

Center for Responsive Politics
1101 14th St. NW, Suite 1030, Washington, DC   20005-5635
(202) 857-0044 • fax: (202) 857-7809
e-mail: info@crp.org

The Center for Responsive Politics is a nonpartisan research group studies the role that money plays in federal elections and researches campaign finance reform issues, such as public funding of election campaigns. The Center for Responsive Politics conducts research on campaign finance issues for the news media and the public at large. It publishes numerous books and booklets, including *Ten Myths About Money in Politics, A Brief History of Money in Politics*, and *Speaking Freely*.

Center for the Study of the American Electorate (CSAE)
421 New Jersey Ave. SE, Washington, DC   20003
(202) 546-3221
Web site: http://spa.american.edu/ccps/pages.php?ID=23

The Center for the Study of the American Electorate (CSAE) provides data and analysis of voter participation, holds a major biennial conference on the state of American democracy, and conduct forums on various issues relating to civic engagement. The CSAE's reports include *Bush, Iraq Propel Modest Turnout Increase Ending 12-Year Republican Revolution: Dems Higher Than Gop For First Time Since 1990* (2006) and *Registration Percentage Unchanged From 2002—Record Percentage Eschew Major Parties* (2006).

Kettering Foundation

444 North Capitol St. NW, Suite 434
Washington, D.C. 20001
(202) 393-4478 • fax: (202) 393-7644

The Kettering Foundation was formed in 1927 as a nonprofit research institution that studies problems of community, governing, politics, and education, with a particular focus on deliberative democracy. It publishes the quarterlies *Kettering Review* and *Connections* newsletter as well as the National Issues Forum book series.

League of Women Voters (LWV)

1730 M St. NW, Suite 1000, Washington, DC 20036-4505
(202) 429-1965 • fax: (202) 429-0854

The League of Women Voters promotes active citizen participation in government and public policy making. Though it does not endorse candidates or political parties, it distributes information on candidates and issues and organizes voter registration and get-out-the-vote drives. The league publishes numerous booklets and pamphlets, including *Wired for Democracy: Using Emerging Technology to Educate Voters, Helping America Vote: Thinking Outside the Ballot Box: Innovations for the Polling Place*, and *Getting the Most Out of Debates.*

Kids Voting USA (KVUSA)

Kids Voting District of Columbia, Tempe, AZ 85282
(480) 921-3727 ext. 203
e-mail: jim@kidsvotingusa.org

Kids Voting USA works to secure the future of democracy by preparing young people to be engaged voters. KVUSA operates through a national network of community-based affiliates that partner with schools and election officials. KVUSA combines classroom instruction, family dialogue, and an authentic voting experience to create a powerful strategy for achieving a long-term change in voting behavior.

National Voting Rights Institute (NVRI)
27 School Street, Suite 500, Boston, MA   02108
(617) 624-3900 • fax: (617) 624-3911

The National Voting Rights Institute is a nonprofit organization that is challenging, through civil lawsuits, the constitutionality of the private financing of public elections. The organization believes that the influence of private money in elections prevents many poorer people from fully participating in the political process.

National Youth Rights Association (NYRA)
1133 19th St. NW, 9th Floor, Washington, DC   20036
Web site: www.youthrights.org

The National Youth Rights Association is a national youth-led organization with over 7,000 members. The NYRA defends the civil rights of young people in the United States through educating people about youth rights and empowering young people to work on their own behalf. The NYRA believes that certain basic rights are an intrinsic part of American citizenship and transcend age.

Twentieth Century Fund
41 E. 70th St., New York, NY   10021
(212) 535-4441 • fax: (212) 535-7534

This research foundation sponsors analyses of economic policy, foreign affairs, and domestic political issues. It publishes numerous books and the report *1-800-PRESIDENT: The Report of the Twentieth Century Fund Task Force on Television and the Campaign of 1992.*

Votes at 16
Chancel Street, London   SE1 0UU
020 7928 1622 • fax: 020 7401 7789
e-mail: info@votesat16.org.uk.

Votes at 16 is a coalition actively campaigning to lower the voting age in Great Britain, working with a broad spectrum of organizations including the Green Party and British Youth

Council. Votes at 16 operates a Web site featuring educational papers designed to help youthful campaigners support their position and circulate petitions.

Bibliography

Books

Alan Abramowitz *Voice of the People: Elections and Voting in the United States.* New York: McGraw-Hill, 2003.

Peter L. Benson *All Kids Are Our Kids: What Communities Must Do to Raise Caring and Responsible Children and Adolescents.* San Francisco: Jossey-Bass, 1997.

Sarah De Capua *Voting.* New York: Children's Press, 2002.

Wendell W. Cultice *Youth's Battle for the Ballot: A History of Voting Age in America* Westport, CT: Greenwood Press, 1992.

Robert C. Fellmeth and Marvin Ventrell *Child Rights & Remedies: How the U.S. Legal System Affects Children.* Atlanta: Clarity Press, 2002.

Martin Guggenheim *What's Wrong with Children's Rights.* Cambridge, MA: Harvard University Press 2005.

Alaimo Kathleen *Children as Equals: Exploring the Rights of the Child.* Lanham, MD: University Press of America, 2002.

Peter Jennings, Todd Brewster, and Jennifer Armstrong *The Century for Young People.* New York City: Doubleday Books for Young Readers, 1999.

Ellen Levine — *Freedom's Children: Young Civil Rights Activists Tell Their Own Stories.* New York: Putnam Juvenile, 2000.

Mark Majka and Linda C. Ensalaco — *Children's Human Rights: Progress and Challenges for Children Worldwide.* New York: Rowman & Littlefield, 2005.

John T. Pardeck — *Children's Rights: Policy And Practice.* Binghamton, NY: Haworth Social Work, 2001.

Thomas E. Patterson — *The Vanishing Voter: Public Involvement in an Age of Uncertainty.* New York: Knopf, 2002.

Nancy E. Walker, Catherine M. Brooks, and Lawrence S. Wrightsman Jr. — *Children's Rights in the United States: In Search of a National Policy.* Thousand Oaks, CA: Sage Publications, Inc, 1999.

Martin P. Wattenberg — *Is Voting for Young People? With a Postscript on Citizen Engagement.* Upper Saddle River, NJ: Longman, 2006.

Periodicals

Elizabeth Cazden — "Old Enough to Fight, Old Enough to Vote," *Cobblestone*, March 2004.

Philip Cowley — "Votes at 16: They All Help the Struggle, Brother," *New Statesman*, April 26, 2004.

Emily Cutler — "Voice Box," *New Moon*, September 1, 2006.

Craig Eisendrath and Miles Orvell — "Making Democracy Work," *USA Today (Magazine)*, September 2005.

"Folly of the 16-Year-Old-Voter" — *Sunday Times*, July 8, 2007.

"Gord Gives Power to the People" — *Daily Record*, July 4, 2007.

"Iran Politicians Woo the Young" — *Christian Science Monitor*, June 16, 2005.

Victor Landauro — "Should the Voting Age Be Lowered?" *Junior Scholastic*, October 27, 2003.

"Let Us Vote! Should States Lower the Voting Age?" — *Know Your World Extra*, October 15, 2004.

Adam Liptak — "1971: 18-Year-Olds Get the Vote," *New York Times Upfront*, September 4, 2006.

"Lowering the Voting Age?" — *Junior Scholastic*, October 2, 2006.

"Lowering Voting Age" — *Herald*, February 28, 2006.

"New Law Lets Teens Serve at Voting Sites" — *Tribune*, November 6, 2006.

Bali Rai — "Now X Marks the Rot," *Times Educational Supplement*, April 29, 2005.

Miranda Rosenberg   "A Campaign to Lower the Voting Age to 16," *New York Times Upfront*, January 12, 2004.

"Teens Who Can't Vote Can Still Help Out on Election Day"   *Daily Herald*, March 17, 2006.

"These Kids Need to Get a Life Not a Vote"   *Mail on Sunday*, July 8, 2007.

"They Vote Yes"   *Los Angeles Times*, May 20, 2004.

"Voice Box"   *New Moon*, Jan–Feb 2007.

"Vote Drives Gain Avid Attention of Youth in '04"   *New York Times*, September 15, 2004.

"Why Shouldn't We Allow Young People the Vote?"   *Western Mail*, March 29, 2006.

"Youth Vote: Why Bother?"   *Youth Today*, Dec/Jan 2003.

Index